NOT YOUR FATHER'S FOUNDERS

AN "AMENDED" LOOK AT AMERICA'S FIRST PATRIOTS

FEDERAL FACTS, REVOLUTIONARY REVELATIONS,
AND QUOTATIONS TO LIVE (*and Die*) BY!

ARTHUR G. SHARP, MA

Adamsmedia
AVON, MASSACHUSETTS

Published by
Adams Media, a division of F+W Media, Inc.
57 Littlefield Street, Avon, MA 02322. U.S.A.
www.adamsmedia.com

ISBN 10: 1-4405-4011-X
ISBN 13: 978-1-4405-4011-0
eISBN 10: 1-4405-4162-0
eISBN 13: 978-1-4405-4162-9

Printed in the United States of America.

10   9   8   7   6   5   4   3   2   1

This publication is designed to provide accurate and authoritative information with regard to the subject matter covered. It is sold with the understanding that the publisher is not engaged in rendering legal, accounting, or other professional advice. If legal advice or other expert assistance is required, the services of a competent professional person should be sought.
—From a *Declaration of Principles* jointly adopted by a Committee of the American Bar Association and a Committee of Publishers and Associations

Many of the designations used by manufacturers and sellers to distinguish their product are claimed as trademarks. Where those designations appear in this book and Adams Media was aware of a trademark claim, the designations have been printed with initial capital letters.

Grunge background and stars © Bigstockphoto.com

This book is available at quantity discounts for bulk purchases.
For information, please call 1-800-289-0963.

Author's Note

Some dates, names, and places given in this book may not agree with those in other historical accounts. That is because record keeping was not an exact science in the eighteenth century. And the British Empire, including its North American colonies, switched calendars in 1752 ("Old Style" versus "New Style") to make sure the new year started on January 1. Consequently, there is often confusion regarding dates of individuals' births and events. For example, depending on the source, Ethan Allen's birth date was January 10, 1738; January 21, 1738; January 21, 1737; or even some other date, depending on the conversion between the Julian and Gregorian calendars. And, he was born in either Litchfield or Roxbury, Connecticut (which is a geography issue, not calendar related). In any case, he was born and lived during the Founding Fathers' era—and performed remarkable feats. Those are the criteria on which this book is based.

CONTENTS

To the brave American men and women who stood up for their rights in the late eighteenth century and contributed to the construction of a new nation— the United States of America.

Acknowledgments

For the efforts of teachers who drum history into students' heads in countless classrooms—even when the students do not think they are listening.

INTRODUCTION

What's All the Fuss About?

The men and women profiled in this book compose a hall of fame of patriots and heroes of the American Revolution. While you may think you've heard all there is to hear about them before, you haven't. The stories in this book are not the typical tales readers are used to hearing about the Founding Fathers and the other people who worked behind the scenes to carry out their revolution.

These offbeat profiles are what make this book unique. More importantly, they'll give you a new perspective on the men and women who founded the country. The founders portrayed here were not always as moral and upright as some histories present them. They had foibles and idiosyncrasies. That's what made them human—and explains why they sometimes acted bizarrely, lived lives of luxury while the country struggled to feed and clothe its army, engaged in scandalous extramarital affairs, etc.

While he was president of the Second Continental Congress in Philadelphia, John Hancock rode around town in an exquisitely decorated chariot, accompanied by fifty armed horsemen and several servants. Benjamin Franklin often defied social mores. In Paris, he played chess late into the night with a close friend of his, a much-younger woman named Madame Brillon de Jouy (1744–1824), while she lay in her bath. Silas Deane may have been murdered, although no one will ever know for sure because his body was buried in an unmarked grave in England and never repatriated. Deborah Sampson was a male impersonator. These are the stories that make this book required reading if you're trying to gain insights into the real personalities of the men and women who created the United States.

Each profile includes a summary of the patriot's life, his or her contributions and achievements, and sidebars that highlight unusual or little-known information. The profiles are listed in alphabetical order because no one was more important than anyone else. All of the people included were instrumental in creating the republic we live in without regard to whose contributions were more significant on a scale of one to ten. Appendix A includes a brief description of the three Acts of King George III and Parliament that inflamed American patriots and spurred them to seek their independence from Britain.

 Quotations to Live (and Die) By!

"GEORGE THE THIRD
OUGHT NEVER TO HAVE OCCURRED.
ONE CAN ONLY WONDER
AT SO GROTESQUE A BLUNDER."
—EDMUND CLERIHEW BENTLEY, BRITISH POET

In these pages, you'll find thinkers and doers, the people who wrote the Constitution, the people who fought to protect it, and the people who upheld it. They include statesmen, spies, scalawags, and soldiers. They came from all walks of life. In the face of hostile laws enacted by the British sovereign, and at great risk to their lives and liberty, they were united in a single purpose: to form an independent United States of America.

Abigail Adams was unique for her time. She was an independent, forward-thinking woman who established a reputation in her own right as a strong, early advocate for women's rights before it was fashionable. She served as a valued adviser to her husband, John Adams, the second president of the United States, on matters of government and politics. Adams also wrote a number of letters that provide contemporary readers with a firsthand account of the Revolutionary War. As First Lady, she was the first to serve as an attack dog for a president, never hesitating to come to her husband's defense regardless of who was criticizing him. She set a precedent for women seeking a contributory role in American society, which separated her from the majority of her female contemporaries and established her own role in history as a women's rights pioneer.

Adams's Youth

Abigail Adams, like most girls of her era, was educated at home. She had a significant advantage over many of the other girls, though. Her father, William Smith, a Congregationalist minister, had a large private library, as did many ministers of the era, who were often the best-educated individuals in eighteenth-century America.

So did her mother's father, John Quincy, who was a member of the colonial governor's council and a militia colonel. The two men instilled in her a love for esoteric subjects such as philosophy, theology, ancient history, government, and law.

Adams was a straight-laced young lady in her youth. By her own admission she did not sing, dance, or play cards. For amusement she read and wrote letters to friends and relatives. Those activities helped prepare her for her life with John, whom she met at her sister Mary's wedding in 1759.

Their courtship was slow. They were married by her father on October 25, 1764, when she was nineteen years old and he was just five days shy of his twenty-ninth birthday. John and Abigail had their first child, named Abigail (or "Nabby"), slightly less than nine months later. Their second child, John Quincy, was born two years later. Altogether, they had three sons and two daughters.

FEDERAL FACTS

John and Abigail's son, John Quincy Adams, became the sixth president of the United States (1825–29). Like his father, he served one term.

Their first few years of marriage were typical of the time. Abigail and John lived in a series of rented houses and eventually bought their own farm, Peacefield, in 1787. But the times were turbulent, and John, who was at the forefront of the colonists' fight for independence, traveled a lot. Abigail was often on her own, which allowed her to build a strong sense of independence. The two developed a reliance on letters to keep them up to date. Neither of them threw away all their letters, which have become a great source of the history of the time.

Quotations to Live (and Die) By!

"THE FLAME IS KINDLED, AND LIKE LIGHTNING IT
CATCHES FROM SOUL TO SOUL."
—ABIGAIL ADAMS TO JOHN ADAMS, NOVEMBER 1773

Once, when Adams was asked for permission to publish some of her political letters, she refused. She considered it improper to release a woman's private correspondence for public consumption. Luckily, a grandson arranged for the 1848 publication of some of her letters. The collection became the first published memoir of a First Lady. The public has been reading Adams's letters ever since.

Political Surveyor

As hostilities between the British and American armies began in 1775, the Massachusetts General Court (the colonial legislature) asked Adams, Adams's close friend Mercy Otis Warren, and Hannah Winthrop to survey women in the colony regarding their Tory (loyal to the king) tendencies. The experience whetted Adams's appetite for political arguments.

Adams began a flood of letters to her husband John to report on her activities as the war progressed. The flood never ended. She never let an opportunity pass to remind John that women were people with the same rights as men. She saw the revolution as a chance for Americans to create a society in which men and women were equal. He listened, but she never convinced him that her opinion on the matter was valid.

Quotations to Live (and Die) By!

"IF PARTICULAR CARE AND ATTENTION IS NOT PAID TO THE LADIES, WE ARE DETERMINED TO FOMENT A REBELLION, AND WILL NOT HOLD OURSELVES BOUND BY ANY LAWS IN WHICH WE HAVE NO VOICE OR REPRESENTATION."
—ABIGAIL ADAMS

Adams's Travels

When John went overseas to England and France, Abigail went along for part of the time to alleviate his loneliness. Even though his political assignments made their separation necessary at times, they took every opportunity to be together. She spent several years in Europe with him from 1784–89, which facilitated his political and social life, especially in France, since he did not speak French well. She was by his side most of the time when he served as vice president (1789–97) and president (1797–1801). Abigail moved with him when the nation's capital was relocated from Philadelphia to Washington in 1800, and she became the first First Lady to inhabit what eventually became known as the White House.

REVOLUTIONARY REVELATIONS

Adams was a reporter for her husband. At a dinner party in Philadelphia when it was still the nation's capital, she sat next to Thomas Jefferson. She pumped him with questions, wrote down the entire conversation later, and handed her notes to John.

During her husband's presidency, she incurred a lot of criticism for her involvement with John's Federalist Party politics. Her husband's political rivals accused her of advocating a war with France, writing pro-administration editorials to friends and relatives and asking them to get the articles published, supporting laws that were unpopular in their views, and promoting public education for women. Their criticisms were as much gender-based as they were political. Abigail Adams was an anomaly at the time because she did not hesitate to speak her mind, which was difficult for some critics to accept.

 Quotations to Live (and Die) By!

"I REGRET THE TRIFLING NARROW CONTRACTED EDUCATION OF THE FEMALES OF MY OWN COUNTRY."

—ABIGAIL ADAMS

Later Life

Abigail did not lose her interest in politics after John lost his 1800 presidential reelection bid to Thomas Jefferson. She acted as a peacekeeper between the two, who developed a serious rift after the campaign. But Abigail did not hold anything back when she told Jefferson what she thought of the dirty politics involved in the election, telling him, "I have never felt any enmity towards you, Sir, for being elected President of the United States. But the instruments made use of and the means which were practised [*sic*] to effect a change have my utter abhorrence and detestation, for they were the blackest calumny and the foulest falsehoods."

For the most part, Adams occupied her time raising her granddaughter Susanna Adams, the daughter of her alcoholic son, Charles, and writing letters to friends, relatives, and political acquaintances. Abigail Adams died of typhoid fever in the seventy-fourth year of her life.

 Quotations to Live (and Die) By!

"THE WHOLE OF HER LIFE HAS BEEN FILLED UP DOING GOOD."

—JOHN ADAMS, AS ABIGAIL LAY DYING

JOHN ADAMS

Quincy, Massachusetts
October 30, 1735–July 4, 1826
One-Third of a Lifetime

In the thirty-five or so years he was active in politics—over one-third of his lifetime—Adams rose from membership in the Massachusetts General Court (the colonial legislature) to delegate to the First and Second Continental Congresses to vice president and then president of the United States. In between he signed the Declaration of Independence, served as the U.S. ambassador to the Netherlands and Britain, and induced France to enter the Revolutionary War on the Americans' side. He made a lot of enemies along the way, but that was a price he was willing to pay.

Becoming a Household Name

John Adams, a Harvard graduate (class of 1755), burst onto the political scene in 1765 when he published *A Dissertation on the Canon and Feudal Law* in opposition to the Stamp Act. The eloquent, yet feisty, words he used in the essay made John Adams a household name around Boston in the 1760s, which was good for his career. His law practice was not paying the bills, but the essay attracted the attention of prominent Bostonians who opposed British policies. They welcomed him into their ranks. The public exposure helped launch his political career.

Quotations to Live (and Die) By!

"LET IT BE KNOWN THAT THE BRITISH LIBERTIES ARE NOT THE GRANTS OF PRINCES OF PARLIAMENTS, BUT ORIGINAL RIGHTS, CONDITIONS OF ORIGINAL CONTRACTS, COEQUAL WITH PREROGATIVE, AND COEVAL WITH GOVERNMENT. THAT MANY OF OUR RIGHTS ARE INHERENT AND ESSENTIAL, AGREED ON AS MAXIMS AND ESTABLISHED AS PRELIMINARIES EVEN BEFORE A PARLIAMENT EXISTED."

—JOHN ADAMS

REVOLUTIONARY REVELATIONS

After passing the bar exam in 1758, Adams had one client in his first year as a lawyer. He did not win his first case at trial until he had been in practice for three years.

His constant agitation against Britain earned him a seat in the provincial legislature in 1770 and a subsequent election to the First Continental Congress in 1774 and the Second Continental Congress in 1775, which carried over into 1776.

The seemingly inexhaustible Adams was one of the driving forces behind the Declaration of Independence. He proposed in 1775 that such a declaration be created and that Thomas Jefferson should write it. Adams served as one of the editors after Jefferson completed his draft. He impressed his political cohorts with his energy, intellect, and

FEDERAL FACTS

John Adams served on approximately ninety different committees and chaired twenty-five of them during the Second Continental Congress.

ambition, but some people had to wonder about his sanity at times. His manic behavior, outspoken demeanor, and lack of tact sometimes exasperated his fellow delegates.

Quotations to Live (and Die) By!

"HE MEANS WELL FOR HIS COUNTRY, IS ALWAYS AN HONEST MAN, OFTEN A WISE ONE, BUT SOMETIMES AND IN SOME THINGS, ABSOLUTELY OUT OF HIS SENSES."

—BENJAMIN FRANKLIN IN A JULY 22, 1783, LETTER TO ROBERT R. LIVINGSTON

What other people thought did not interest Adams. He had a country to help build, and he was willing to do whatever it took, even if it went against his principles occasionally. For instance, he did not protest when the Congress eliminated any condemnation of slavery from the final version of the Declaration of Independence, even though he fiercely opposed the practice. As he told fellow patriot and congressional delegate Benjamin Rush, "I will see it out, or go to heaven in its ruins." He did not slow down once the document was signed and the Revolutionary War expanded.

Ten Years Overseas

Congress needed a diplomat to keep the French on the Americans' side. Silas Deane, Benjamin Franklin, and Arthur Lee represented the United States in Paris, but they were not well suited to working together effectively. Lee was seldom ready to work before 11 A.M., in contrast to Franklin; Lee accused Deane and Franklin of siphoning off some of the money they were supposed to use to buy arms from the French. Franklin allegedly was more interested in socializing than negotiating a treaty of alliance.

Congress dispatched Adams in February 1778 to restore peace and harmony. By the time he arrived in Paris, a Treaty of Amity and Commerce negotiated by Franklin, Lee, and Deane had already been signed. Nevertheless, he remained in Europe, finalizing a pact of assistance with the French and soliciting loan and trade agreements with the Dutch. Neither activity earned him a ticket home. He was too valuable in Europe.

With unusual tact, diplomacy, and energy, Adams worked to draw up the Treaty of Paris that ended the Revolutionary War.

REVOLUTIONARY REVELATIONS

John Adams returned to America once during the Revolutionary War. He was at home on a working vacation from July to November 1779. While there, he helped draft the Massachusetts Constitution of 1780.

He stayed in Europe as a diplomat and minister to England until 1788. He was alone for about half of the ten years he was overseas. Abigail and their daughter Nabby joined him in 1784, while his other children remained in Massachusetts to complete their studies.

Abigail and Nabby's presence made his life more bearable. The tranquility they brought him would not last.

Life at the Top

The face of politics in America had changed after the ratification of the U.S. Constitution in 1788. There was a split among those who wanted a strong federal government (Federalists) with limited citizen involvement and those who preferred a weak one (Democratic-Republicans). Adams got into the middle of the fight. He believed in a strong federal government, but he did not discount the citizens' role in it. Adams wanted them to be as engaged in the politics and welfare of their country as he was. He served as George Washington's vice president for two terms, then won his own term as president in 1796.

John Adams was the first president to live in the Executive Mansion, which did not become officially known as the White House until 1902, during the presidency of Theodore Roosevelt.

Adams had a turbulent four years. Two issues dominated his presidency: the Quasi-War with France and the unpopular Alien and Sedition Acts.

FEDERAL FACTS

The Federalists dominated U.S. politics through George Washington's two terms as president. Their opposition, the Democratic-Republicans, came into prominence around 1792 and grew stronger after Adams's presidency ended in 1801.

The Alien and Sedition Acts

The Alien and Sedition Acts comprised four laws passed in 1798 in anticipation of war with France. They increased the waiting period for naturalization, authorized the expulsion of aliens who were considered dangerous, and curtailed press criticism of the U.S. government.

Although the acts expired or were repealed by 1802, they killed Adams's chances of reelection in 1800. Thomas Jefferson, who had opposed the Alien and Sedition Acts, won the election. Adams not only lost the presidency, but he temporarily lost Jefferson as a friend. They reconciled in 1812.

REVOLUTIONARY REVELATIONS

Thomas Jefferson and John Adams died on the same day: July 4, 1826. Allegedly, Adams's last words were, "Thomas Jefferson survives." Unbeknownst to him, Jefferson had died a few hours earlier.

Adams spent the last quarter of his life at their farm, Peacefield, with Abigail and their children and grandchildren. The man who had traveled so much to build a country seldom left home after 1801.

JOHN QUINCY ADAMS

Quincy, Massachusetts
July 11, 1767–February 23, 1848
His Father's Son

John Quincy Adams was the only Founding Father's son to become president of the United States. He was well qualified, even if he did not live up to many people's expectations. In his early years in politics he served as a minister to the Netherlands, Portugal, Prussia, Russia, and Britain. Later, he was a Massachusetts state senator, U.S. senator, U.S. congressman, peace and commerce treaty negotiator, secretary of state, and U.S. president. Sadly, his mother, Abigail, did not live to see him become president.

Like Father, Like Son

Ideally, the best way for a Founding Father to make sure the ideas of his generation were carried over to succeeding generations was to inculcate them in a son. That way, the son would act as a conduit. It did not quite work out that way for John Adams and his son, John Quincy Adams.

REVOLUTIONARY REVELATIONS

John Quincy Adams watched the 1775 Battle of Bunker Hill from the family's farm when he was seven years old. It had a chilling effect on him, as he described in a March 1846 letter. It terrified his mother and placed him and his family in "unintermitted danger" from that point on.

By the time he was fifteen years old, he had visited more places and done more things than most people several times his age. He accompanied his father to Europe in 1768 and 1780, traveled to Russia, began his studies at the University of Leiden in the Netherlands, and participated as an "additional secretary" in the peace talks in Paris to end the Revolutionary War.

Throughout his life, he worked to expand on his father's and his contemporaries' visions of a strong republic, although he did not always agree with his father's political views. He had many opportunities to accomplish the mission.

 Quotations to Live (and Die) By!

"ALL MEN PROFESS HONESTY AS LONG AS THEY CAN. TO BELIEVE ALL MEN HONEST WOULD BE FOLLY. TO BELIEVE NONE SO IS SOMETHING WORSE."

—JOHN QUINCY ADAMS

By the time he graduated from Harvard in 1787 and passed his bar exam three years later, he was an experienced diplomat. President George Washington took advantage of his experience.

John Q. the Minister

In May 1794, Washington appointed Adams the U.S. minister to the Netherlands, then transferred him to Portugal. After John Adams was elected president, he redirected his son to Berlin in 1797, where he negotiated a treaty of amity and commerce with Prussia.

His ministerial career came to an abrupt halt in 1801 after Thomas Jefferson became president. John Quincy returned to the United States and applied his talents to politics, starting his legislative career as a state senator. In 1803 he was elected to the U.S. Senate. He broke away from his father's Federalist Party once there. He sided with the Democratic-Republicans on issues such as the Louisiana Purchase and a trade embargo against Britain.

Quotations to Live (and Die) By!

"AMERICA DOES NOT GO ABROAD IN SEARCH OF MONSTERS TO DESTROY. SHE IS THE WELL-WISHER TO FREEDOM AND INDEPENDENCE OF ALL. SHE IS THE CHAMPION AND VINDICATOR ONLY OF HER OWN."
—JOHN QUINCY ADAMS

That was contrary to the wishes of the people of Massachusetts and resulted in the state holding a special election several months before his term was scheduled to end. He lost the election and resigned from the Senate to become a professor of rhetoric and oratory at Harvard.

Quotations to Live (and Die) By!

"ALWAYS VOTE FOR PRINCIPLE, THOUGH YOU MAY VOTE ALONE, AND YOU MAY CHERISH THE SWEETEST REFLECTION THAT YOUR VOTE IS NEVER LOST."
—JOHN QUINCY ADAMS

He switched to the Democratic-Republican Party and resumed his political career after his three-year hiatus as a teacher.

His father's old—and growing older—friends continued to advance John Quincy's career. President Madison named him as minister to Russia, a post he filled from 1809–14. Next, he accepted the same post in Britain, where he served from 1815–17.

Adams did not stay in England long. He returned to the United States in 1817. President James Monroe appointed him as secretary of state. That opened the door for Adams to participate in two major events: the 1820 acquisition of Florida and the 1823 implementation of the Monroe Doctrine, which warned European powers for the first time to keep their distance from the United States' sphere of influence, which included South America and the Caribbean islands.

FEDERAL FACTS

John Adams, John Quincy Adams, and his son, Charles Francis Adams, all served as ministers to Great Britain during their careers.

REVOLUTIONARY REVELATIONS

Even though the Monroe Doctrine is attributed to James Monroe, historians credit John Quincy Adams with being the true architect of the policy.

The Second President Adams

Adams campaigned to replace Monroe after Monroe's second term ended. Adams entered a four-candidate race in which he ran second to Andrew Jackson in the popular election. Because no one achieved a majority of the popular or electoral votes, the House of Representatives cast the deciding vote.

The House of Representatives voted for Adams. Jackson was convinced that Adams had promised Henry Clay—a member of the U.S. House of Representatives, an unsuccessful candidate for president, and a political ally of John Quincy Adams—a position as secretary of state in exchange for using his influence to woo House members to vote for Adams. Jackson called it a "corrupt bargain" and withdrew his support for Adams during his presidency. The feud that developed between Jackson and

Adams as a result prevented Adams from accomplishing anything significant during his term, since Jackson's followers in Congress refused to support the president's initiatives. Jackson ran against Adams again in 1828 on an anticorruption platform and won election by a wide margin.

John Quincy Adams returned to Massachusetts to retire. His retirement did not last long. Like his parents, he did not have the patience to sit and do nothing when there were constituents to serve.

FEDERAL FACTS

In the 1824 presidential election, Andrew Jackson won 43.1 percent of the popular vote and 99 of the 261 available Electoral College votes. Adams got 30.5 percent and 84 votes respectively. The other two candidates, William Crawford and Henry Clay, split the rest almost evenly. Since no one candidate had a majority of electoral votes, the decision as to who would be president fell into the hands of the U.S. House of Representatives.

 Quotations to Live (and Die) By!

"PATIENCE AND PERSEVERANCE HAVE A MAGICAL EFFECT BEFORE WHICH DIFFICULTIES DISAPPEAR AND OBSTACLES VANISH."

—JOHN QUINCY ADAMS

Any bitter feelings he experienced following the presidential election of 1828 dissipated after the people of Massachusetts elected him to the U.S. House of Representatives in 1830.

For the next eighteen years, John Quincy Adams concentrated on abolishing slavery. At first, he was like a man with laryngitis whispering into a gale force wind: Nobody heard his message. Gradually, he started winning converts. By the time his tenure in Congress—and his life—came to a close, he had made significant progress in bringing about the end of slavery.

Adams did not live to see it happen. He suffered a stroke in the House of Representatives on February 21, 1848, and died two days later.

It was a fitting end for a man who strived diligently to uphold the virtues and goals of his father and his contemporaries: His political career ended in a legislative building as he was fighting for what he and they believed in so strongly.

SAMUEL ADAMS

Boston, Massachusetts
September 27, 1722–October 2, 1803
Liberty, Not Beer

Samuel Adams was a master politician—literally. He earned a master of arts degree from Harvard at age twenty-one and ultimately worked as a tax collector. Because he was a disaster as a businessman, he had to do something in the public realm. Using his political skills, he occupied seats in the Massachusetts Assembly and in the First and Second Continental Congresses. He was a signer of the Declaration of Independence, a delegate to the Massachusetts state constitutional convention in 1781, and lieutenant governor and governor of Massachusetts. He never made good beer, though.

Starting Out

Like many young men of his era, Adams struggled trying to find an occupation that suited him. It was difficult for him to find a lasting job because he was obsessed with politics and colonial independence.

A growing number of colonists were distraught with British taxation policies leading up to the Revolutionary War. Adams was among them; he considered the policies taxation without representation. Ironically, he was a tax collector.

The Boston Town Meeting elected Samuel Adams as a tax collector in 1756, but he made a mess of that job. He frequently failed to collect taxes owed. By 1764, his accounts were short more than £8,000, and he was out of the job. Eventually, Adams and some of his friends paid part of the missing funds and the town meeting wrote off the rest.

REVOLUTIONARY REVELATIONS

Samuel Adams's father was a merchant and brewer. Young Samuel worked for a while at the family brewery, but he did not have the head for it—or for business in general.

Have Faith in Samuel

Samuel Adams did not become an active opponent of British taxation policies until 1763, when the citizens of Boston formed a committee to let the king and Parliament know how they felt about the new levies. They appointed Samuel Adams to the committee, putting him in the ironic position of protesting British-imposed taxes while he was collecting them. Nevertheless, he accepted the honor with relish and developed

FEDERAL FACTS

Samuel Adams's 1743 master's thesis was based on this question: "Whether it be lawful to resist the supreme magistrate, if the commonwealth cannot be otherwise preserved?"

He pursued the answer for the next thirty-three years, answering it with finality when he signed the Declaration of Independence.

some pointed rebukes to the British, such as this one: "If our trade may be taxed, why not our lands? Why not the produce of our lands, and every thing we possess, or use? This we conceive annihilates our charter rights to govern and tax ourselves."

Adams's eloquent arguments raised his stature in the citizens' eyes. They looked at him as their protester-in-chief, and he justified their faith in him. As he grew bolder in his attacks on the British, the people of Boston rewarded him by electing him to the Massachusetts General Court in

1765. That gave him a broad forum from which to lead the protests. He became almost a one-person legislature. He was appointed Clerk of the Court, which gave him the opportunity to attend every committee meeting, write the reports, and exert his influence on virtually anything the legislature did. He also produced numerous political essays for consumption outside the court, urging citizens to make their voices heard.

FEDERAL FACTS

While Samuel Adams was a member of the Massachusetts General Court, he suggested that the colonies set up a meeting in New York to discuss their grievances. It took ten years for the idea to take hold, but his idea led to the formation of the First Continental Congress.

The Boston Massacre in 1770 and the Tea Party in 1773 inflamed the increasingly restless people of Boston. After each event, Samuel Adams exhorted the people to continue their opposition to Britain. The Boston Town Meeting organized an economic boycott of British goods in May 1774. Samuel Adams was at the forefront of the plan. He set the example; they followed his leadership.

Thomas Jefferson credited Samuel Adams with being the linchpin of the Congress. He noted, "If there was any Palinurus (helmsman) to the Revolution, Samuel Adams was the man." When the delegates lined up to sign the Declaration of Independence, Adams added his name to the list.

During the War

Adams continued working tirelessly for the United States during the Revolutionary War.

As was his custom, Adams worked with many committees to keep his hand in what was going on. One of his most important assignments was with the Board of War, to which he was appointed in 1777. His background came in handy in that function.

Quotations to Live (and Die) By!

"HE EATS LITTLE, DRINKS LITTLE, SLEEPS LITTLE, THINKS MUCH, AND IS MOST INDEFATIGABLE IN THE PURSUIT OF HIS OBJECT. IT WAS THIS MAN, WHO BY HIS SUPERIOR APPLICATION, MANAGED AT ONCE THE FACTIONS IN CONGRESS AT PHILADELPHIA, AND THE FACTIONS OF NEW ENGLAND."

—JOSEPH GALLOWAY

The Board of War's role was to oversee the Continental Army's administration and make recommendations to Congress on how to improve its operations. Adams had many ideas, such as paying bonuses to soldiers to induce them to reenlist and confiscating the property of Tories. He could not tolerate Tories during or after the war. Adams believed they would destroy the new government the Americans had worked so hard to form.

Quotations to Live (and Die) By!

"ALL MIGHT BE FREE IF THEY VALUED FREEDOM, AND DEFENDED IT AS THEY SHOULD."

—SAMUEL ADAMS

Adams stayed in Congress until 1781. Finally, he resigned and went home to resume his political career in Massachusetts.

Welcome Home, Governor

The people of Massachusetts welcomed Adams with open arms, and immediately elected him to the state Senate. He served as president of the body from 1782–85 and 1787–88. There were two more offices ahead for him: lieutenant governor and governor.

Samuel Adams served as lieutenant governor of Massachusetts from 1789–93, became acting governor in 1793 after John Hancock died in office, and was elected governor from 1794–97.

Ironically, Adams was not pleased with the federal government that emerged after the fight for independence ended. He was especially unhappy with the U.S. Constitution, primarily because of the strong central government it proposed and the lack of rights it afforded individuals. Once he was satisfied that a Bill of Rights would be included, he voted for the document at the Massachusetts ratifying convention. His support turned the tide in the state. (Massachusetts narrowly ratified the U.S. Constitution on a vote of 187–168.)

Quotations to Live (and Die) By!

"I CONFESS, AS I ENTER THE BUILDING I STUMBLE AT THE THRESHOLD. I MEET WITH A NATIONAL GOVERN- MENT, INSTEAD OF A FEDERAL UNION OF STATES."
—SAMUEL ADAMS TO RICHARD HENRY LEE, 1787

Adams retired from politics after his final term as governor ended in 1797. The man Thomas Jefferson called "the Father of the Revolution" left behind an unparalleled record of achievements—even though he had never mastered the art of brewing beer.

☙ ETHAN ALLEN ☙

Litchfield, Connecticut
January 21, 1738–February 12, 1789
An Overrated Historical Figure

Ethan Allen showed Americans that they could beat the British in military battles. He led the Green Mountain Boys' assault on Fort Ticonderoga in May 1775, where they captured the artillery the troops in Boston used to drive the British army out of the city. That was his only significant contribution to the Revolutionary War, but it etched his name in American history.

Sparring for Land

After his father died in 1755, Ethan took over the management of the family farm, which short-circuited his education. Two years later, he joined the militia to participate in the ongoing French and Indian War (1754–63), but didn't see any action. In 1769, Ethan and his brothers acquired some land in the New Hampshire Grants, despite the fact that the ownership of the land (and thus the legal ability to grant it) had actually been given to New York by King George. The New York provincial government attempted to exert its authority in the disputed area, demanding additional payment to validate ownership of the lands.

Local lads formed their own militia to fight off New Yorkers who tried to take what they thought was theirs. These locals called themselves the "Green Mountain Boys" and chose Allen as their leader.

Quotations to Live (and Die) By!

"Ever since I arrived to a state of manhood and acquainted myself with the general history of mankind, I have felt a sincere passion for liberty."
—Ethan Allen

As a result of their frequent skirmishes with the New Yorkers, Allen's militia members were combat veterans by the time the Revolutionary War began.

Taking Ticonderoga

General George Washington needed artillery to help him drive the British army out of Boston. Benedict Arnold (among others) knew where there was some for the taking: Fort Ticonderoga in New York.

The Massachusetts Committee of Safety authorized Benedict Arnold to raise a force of 400 men and lead it to Fort Ticonderoga.

The Connecticut Committee of Public Safety asked Ethan Allen and Captain Edward Mott and their 200–300 soldiers to join with Arnold to capture the fort. Everyone met at Lake Champlain to complete the mission. There was one problem: Who would lead the attack?

Allen and Arnold both had egos the size of a New Hampshire Land Grant, each of which was about six miles square. They argued about who should lead the troops.

Eventually both swallowed their high opinions of themselves and compromised: They would share command.

On May 10, 1775, Allen, Arnold, and eighty-three troops approached Fort Ticonderoga at dawn. They surprised the British troops and captured the fort without firing a shot and without any injuries.

The Americans captured the cannons and shipped them to Boston. Arnold and Allen picked their next target: Fort St. John, at the northern end of Lake Champlain. Allen's part in the raid turned into a comedy of errors.

Prisoner of War

Arnold and fifty of his troops boarded a schooner armed with swivel guns and sailed toward the fort. Allen and 100 men loaded into four oar- and sail-powered boats to reach the fort. It was a four-day trip, for which Allen did not prepare adequately. He neglected to pack enough food for the attack. Not surprisingly, Arnold reached the fort first, captured it, and headed back to his new headquarters at Crown Point. He met Allen and his "armada" en route; they were still rowing toward Fort St. John. Arnold and Allen greeted one another, drank a couple toasts to Arnold's success, and went their separate ways.

Next, Allen traveled to Philadelphia to ask Congress to include the Green Mountain Boys in the Continental Army. Congress did—but rejected Allen as the Green Mountain Boys' leader. Uncharacteristically, Allen accepted the rebuke and accompanied the regiment in its Canadian invasion as a civilian scout. He was captured on September 25, 1775, by the British, and held as a prisoner until 1778. Even the American commander of the expedition was happy about Allen's predicament.

 Quotations to Live (and Die) By!
"I AM VERY APPREHENSIVE OF DISAGREEABLE CONSEQUENCES ARISING FROM MR. ALLEN'S IMPRUDENCE. I ALWAYS DREADED HIS IMPATIENCE AND IMPRUDENCE."
—AMERICAN GENERAL PHILIP SCHUYLER REGARDING ETHAN ALLEN'S CAPTURE

The war went on without Allen. After he was included in a general prisoner exchange in May 1778, he joined General George Washington's forces at Valley Forge, Pennsylvania. Washington applauded Allen and told him he would be in touch, which was just as much a brushoff then as it is today.

REVOLUTIONARY REVELATIONS

The Continental Army awarded Allen with the brevetted (temporary) rank of colonel and payment of $75 a month. He was never activated, and his payments gradually disappeared.

Welcome Home

Allen had been away from Vermont for so long that he did not realize it had declared independence in 1777. The following year, Vermont enacted a Banishment Act that allowed the republic to seize and sell the property owned by Tories. The republic was busily confiscating property owned by Tories within its borders. This created the perfect job opening for Allen, who received an appointment as a judge to determine who qualified as a Tory. He even escorted some of the people found guilty of being Tories to New York to be handed over to British authorities. His judgeship did not last long, but he kept finding Tories on his own and turning them over to officials.

Between 1780 and his death in 1789, Allen wrote books and poems, remarried after his first wife's death, and sold his land. Allen almost ended up in debtors' prison a couple times, but he managed to squeak by until he died after a stroke.

REVOLUTIONARY REVELATIONS

Ethan Allen reported his brother Levi to a Board of Confiscation, whose job it was to seize and dispose of Tories' property to raise revenues for the republic. Though Levi had tried to secure Ethan's release from British captivity during his three-year incarceration, it's possible that he might have been trying to swindle Ethan and another brother out of some land when Ethan turned him in. They reconciled in 1783.

Allen's original grave marker disappeared in the 1850s. The Vermont legislature authorized a replacement, which was placed in the graveyard where he is buried. But the exact location of his grave is unknown. Moreover, there is no known likeness of Ethan Allen in existence. That is fitting: The country had enough trouble dealing with the original.

PENELOPE BARKER

Penelope Padgett Hodgson Craven Barker was one of the first women of the Revolutionary era to make a public statement about the outrageous behavior of King George and his Parliament. In October 1774 she hosted a tea party in Edenton, North Carolina, where fifty-one women signed a pledge to boycott tea and other manufactured goods sent to the colonies from Britain. Her name does not appear in many history books, but her role in the history of the American rebellion should not be underestimated.

The Richest Woman in North Carolina

North Carolina was a hotbed of opposition to Britain. While the patriots in Boston were getting most of the press, the citizens of North Carolina were fomenting a revolution of their own. Penelope Barker spearheaded a boycott movement among women throughout the colonies—and she was not afraid to take a jab at men.

Barker was not a neophyte when it came to politics. She had spent a considerable amount of time around the leading politicians of Edenton during her childhood and three marriages. Her father was a prominent doctor and planter who taught her management skills and the need for personal responsibility. Her marriages reinforced those lessons.

Quotations to Live (and Die) By!

"MAYBE IT HAS ONLY BEEN MEN WHO HAVE PROTESTED THE KING UP TO NOW. THAT ONLY MEANS WE WOMEN HAVE TAKEN TOO LONG TO LET OUR VOICES BE HEARD. WE ARE SIGNING OUR NAMES TO A DOCUMENT, NOT HIDING OURSELVES BEHIND COSTUMES LIKE THE MEN IN BOSTON DID AT THEIR TEA PARTY. THE BRITISH WILL KNOW WHO WE ARE."

—PENELOPE BARKER

She married in 1745 for the first time to John Hodgson (or Hodges), who had been married to her sister Elizabeth. He died soon after, and left Penelope as a nineteen-year-old pregnant widow with his and Elizabeth's two children, one of their own, and another one on the way.

Barker inherited a significant amount of land from Hodgson, which was uncommon at the time. Normally, widows received one-third of their deceased husbands' estates, primarily to enhance their chances of attracting another husband. That worked in Penelope Barker's case.

Husband number two was James Craven, a wealthy planter. He, too, left his entire estate to Barker.

The deaths of two husbands by the time she was only twenty-eight did not dissuade her from marrying a third time. After all, she was—at that young age—the richest woman in North Carolina. Attorney Thomas Barker became her third husband, with whom she had three more children.

Thomas traveled to England on business quite often. Penelope managed their affairs while he was gone, which gave her some valuable insights into the political realities of the time. Thomas was gone on one trip for seventeen years! He sailed to London in 1761 to serve as agent for the North Carolina colony. There was a British blockade of American ships in place at the time, which prevented him from returning to North Carolina. He finally made it back in 1778, long after Penelope's party ended.

Not the Typical Tea Party

Penelope Barker did not see why the men of North Carolina should bear the burden of rebellion during this tumultuous time. Her female friends agreed with her. Barker invited many of them to a tea party at the home of Elizabeth King to sign a document she had written proclaiming their intention to boycott British goods.

Quotations to Live (and Die) By!

"WE THE LADYES OF EDENTON DO HEREBY SOLEMNLY ENGAGE NOT TO CONFORM TO YE PERNICIOUS CUSTOM OF DRINKING TEA OR THAT WE, THE AFORESAID LADYES, WILL NOT PROMOTE YE WEAR OF ANY MANUFACTURE FROM ENGLAND, UNTIL SUCH TIME THAT ALL ACTS WHICH TEND TO ENSLAVE THIS OUR NATIVE COUNTRY SHALL BE REPEALED."

—PENELOPE BARKER'S PETITION

Barker was ahead of her time in recognizing the value of good public relations. She sent a copy of her declaration to a London newspaper, which published it in the form of text and cartoons lampooning their boycott. Consequently, the meeting and the boycott drew a lot of attention in the city. That was not surprising, since newspapers there portrayed Barker and her friends as bad mothers and loose women. Their ad hominem attack did not stop the women back in the colonies from supporting the ladies of Edenton.

Women in several other locations in America launched their own boycotts. The negative impact on the British economy got the attention of the king and Parliament, even if the Edenton Tea Party declaration did not.

Penelope Barker's appearance on the Revolutionary-era stage was brief. Eventually, the furor over her Tea Party document subsided. Her impact on the rebellion did not. She died in 1796 at age sixty-eight, but she will always be remembered as a leader who encouraged other women to get involved openly in the American movement for independence.

FEDERAL FACTS

Penelope Barker's October 25, 1774, tea party was reputedly the first women's political rally in America. There may have been others, but they did not get the publicity Barker's did.

Although Penelope Barker gets most of the credit for the Edenton Tea Party, it took courage for all the women to sign the document. No doubt the fact that many of them were related to one another buoyed their courage due to moral support. They all deserve public acknowledgement. Here are their names:

- Anne Anderson
- Penelope Barker
- Sarah Beasley
- Elizabeth Beasely
- Ruth Benbury
- Lydia Bennet
- Jean Blair
- Mary Blount
- Rebecca Bondfield
- Lydia Bonner
- Mary Bonner
- Margaret Cathcart
- Abigale Charlton
- Grace Clayton
- Elizabeth Creacy
- Mary Creacy
- Elizabeth Crickett
- Tresia Cunningham
- Penelope Dawson
- Elizabeth Green
- Anne Hall
- Frances Hall
- Anne Haughton
- Sarah Hoskins
- Anne Horniblow
- Sarah Howe
- Sarah Howcott
- Mary Hunter
- Elizabeth Johnston
- Anne Johnstone

- F. Johnstone
- Mary Jones
- Mary Littedle
- Sarah Littlejohn
- Sarah Mathews
- Elizabeth P. Ormond
- M. Payne
- Elizabeth Patterson
- Margaret Pearson
- Mary Ramsay
- Elizabeth Roberts
- Elizabeth Vail
- Susannah Vail
- Sarah Valentine
- Marion Wells
- Jane Wellwood
- Mary Woolard

For a young man from rural New Hampshire, a large city like Philadelphia in 1776 must have seemed like a foreign country. The entire population of New Hampshire at that time was around 80,000 people. There were 30,000 in Philadelphia. Yet Josiah Bartlett had the courage and credentials to travel to the big city alone and take his seat at the Continental Congress that year for the sake of independence. Bartlett was not the rural bumpkin stereotype that people in more culturally advanced places such as Boston pictured. He knew Latin and Greek, was a physician, a colonel in the militia, and a justice of the peace. Bartlett was a well-rounded man, just the kind New Hampshire needed to represent it at the Continental Congress. He had a reputation as a principled individual and legislator who was willing to defy pro-British authorities such as the royal governor. He did not disappoint the people of his state.

A Whig Gets Into the Governor's Hair

Josiah Bartlett began his political career in the tiny frontier town of Kingston, New Hampshire. There were few families living there, and he was the only doctor in the area. Since he was well educated, people looked to him for guidance in political and health matters. It was not surprising that they elected him to the Colonial Assembly in 1765.

REVOLUTIONARY REVELATIONS

Bartlett was married on January 15, 1754. There is some question about whom he married. Local records show that he was married to a Mary Bartlett. Genealogy documents at the Harvard Library list his wife as his cousin, Hannah Webster. Either way, he and his wife had twelve children, three of whom became doctors—as did seven of their grandsons.

As the colonists began to express their dissatisfaction with British policies, Bartlett became more vocal about his Whig views.

Whigs were anti-king and Parliament. They were opposed by the Tories. Bartlett's views put him on a collision course with New Hampshire's royal governor, John Wentworth—a course that would end well only for one of them. It was not Wentworth.

Dueling Assemblies

Like many of his patriot brethren, Bartlett got his start in the Continental Congress through the Committee of Correspondence, which he joined in 1774 while serving in New Hampshire's Assembly. Wentworth learned that year about the formation of a committee of correspondence appointed by the assembly to promote independence for New Hampshire and coordinate its efforts with similar groups from other colonies. Consequently, he dissolved the assembly. Undeterred, the disbanded delegates formed their own Provincial Assembly.

FEDERAL FACTS

It was common among the colonies at the time for members of dissolved general assemblies to form their own legislative bodies in defiance of their governors. Then, the rogue, extralegal assemblies would select delegates to the Continental Congress.

The New Hampshire Provincial Assembly immediately appointed Bartlett as one of its two delegates to the First Continental Congress. He turned down the assignment "to spend more time with his family." (That much-loved excuse is older than you may think!) However, it's possible that Bartlett stayed in New Hampshire to protect his family; his home had burned down under mysterious circumstances in 1774. The Tories were prime suspects. By a strange coincidence, the home of the other delegate, John Pickering, also burned down that same year.

Political bickering in New Hampshire came to a head in 1775. Patriots expelled Governor Wentworth, but he did not leave without a fight. One of his final acts was to revoke Bartlett's commissions as justice of the peace, colonel, and assemblyman. It was a desperate act by a disappointed man. The Provincial Assembly responded by appointing Bartlett to represent the colony at the Second Continental Congress in 1775 and 1776.

A Busy Bartlett

1775 was a difficult year for Bartlett. He was the only delegate from New Hampshire at the Second Continental Congress for a while. Because Congress preferred that each of its committees include at least one representative from each colony, Bartlett was kept very busy serving on the committees considered most important: safety, secrecy, munitions, marine. If there was a committee of significance, Bartlett was on it.

Finally, Bartlett wrote home in desperation to ask for help. The Provincial Assembly dispatched John Langdon and William Whipple to complement Bartlett. Whipple was back the next year to sign the Declaration of Independence, along with Bartlett and Matthew Thornton.

Once Bartlett's workload decreased, he threw himself into the congressional committee activities in Philadelphia to the point that both his mental and physical health weakened, although he recovered quickly.

REVOLUTIONARY REVELATIONS

Josiah Bartlett was the first delegate asked whether independence from Britain was a good idea. The Second Continental Congress accorded him that honor when it decided to begin the polling with the northernmost colony and proceed geographically to the southern delegations. He answered yes. In that same vein, when the delegates to the Second Continental Congress signed the Declaration of Independence on August 2, 1776, Bartlett was the second signer, after John Hancock.

After the Congress concluded its mission, Bartlett returned to New Hampshire, but his work was far from done.

Age Before Duty

As a reward for his hard work, the New Hampshire Assembly reelected Bartlett to another term with the Continental Congress. This time he abstained. His wife, who had managed the family farm and raised the children in his absence, was as tired as he was. He served one more term in the Continental Congress in 1778 and then returned to New Hampshire to retire—sort of.

REVOLUTIONARY REVELATIONS

Dr. Josiah Bartlett applied his medical skills at the August 16, 1777, Battle of Bennington. Even though it was named for a town in Vermont, the battle actually took place at Walloomsac, New York, ten miles west. Other than that one battle, Bartlett did not participate in the war.

Bartlett could not sit around. He held almost every political office in New Hampshire while continuing his medical practice. He served as the chief justice of the New Hampshire Supreme Court—even though he was not a lawyer—and governor. The state legislature selected him to serve as a U.S. senator, but he turned down the position because it required him to leave New Hampshire.

But Josiah Bartlett could not go on forever. His dual medical and political careers took their toll on his health. He resigned from the governor's chair in 1794 and died a year later.

Bartlett, like so many of his cosigners, is remembered via the names of towns and streets in New Hampshire. But there is no more vivid memory of him than his signature on the Declaration of Independence. That was a big honor for the man from the small colony of New Hampshire.

WILLIAM CAMPBELL

Augusta, Virginia
1745–August 22, 1781
A Campbell Created by a Committee

Brigadier General and political leader William Campbell's role in the Revolutionary War was like a cameo in a movie. Few people recognize his name or his role. He and his troops defeated a Tory army at Kings Mountain, North Carolina, on October 7, 1780, in a relatively obscure battle that had a large impact on the outcome of the war and the country's future. He was a symbol of the virtually unrecognized men and women who stepped up during the war and made contributions that did not seem important at the time, but that altered the course of history.

Tories Be Terrorized

Campbell was a member of the Virginia House of Burgesses (the colony's legislature, which was the first assembly of elected representatives of English colonists in North America), like his brother-in-law Patrick Henry, a patriot who despised British rule.

On January 20, 1775, Campbell, along with twelve other representatives of Fincastle County, Virginia, signed a resolution to be forwarded to the colony's delegation at the First Continental Congress. It stated that they would resist the Intolerable Acts (punitive laws of the British—see Appendix A for more information). They swore they would fight to their deaths to preserve their political liberties. The document became known as the Fincastle Resolutions.

Campbell was willing to do more than sign resolutions. He was ready and willing to fight the British, wherever and whenever. He was especially eager to punish Tories for their misguided allegiance if the chance arose. It did.

> ## REVOLUTIONARY REVELATIONS
> Campbell was not fond of Tories. He earned the nickname of the "bloody tyrant of Washington County" for his harsh treatment of people who remained loyal to Britain during the war.

King of Kings Mountain

State militias in the southern part of the United States were busy between 1778 and 1781. The British invaded the region because they believed the numerous Tories in the area would flock to their side. They did not reckon on the strength and cunning of the patriots, who fought an unconventional battle at Kings Mountain, North Carolina, just west of Charlotte.

The Battle of Kings Mountain, which is omitted or glossed over in many history books, is considered by some historians as the turning point in the Revolutionary War. The patriot militia's victory destroyed the left wing of General Charles Cornwallis's British army and forced it to abandon its operations in North Carolina. Cornwallis moved his army to South Carolina to await reinforcements. While he waited, American General Nathanael Greene increased his own forces, which were ultimately successful in driving Cornwallis out of South Carolina as well.

The Battle of Kings Mountain did not involve regular British troops. It was fought between patriot and Tory militia units. The Tories were led by Major Patrick Ferguson, a Scottish officer in the British army—and the only regular army officer on either side at the battle.

The American forces that convened at Kings Mountain included about 900 troops led by Campbell, John Sevier, Isaac Shelby, Benjamin Cleveland, Charles McDowell, and James Williams. They combined their forces when they arrived for the battle, but they did not have a chief commander. They put the matter to a vote. Campbell became the overall commander of the patriot forces—in other words, a leader created by a committee.

Major Ferguson's little army included about 1,125 Tories defending a mountain about one-quarter mile long at an elevation slightly above 1,003 feet. He was confident in his ability to ward off any patriot attack. Ferguson was wrong. The patriots were determined to drive the enemy off the mountain—if any of the Tories were still alive after the battle.

 Quotations to Live (and Die) By!

"HE WAS ON KINGS MOUNTAIN, THAT HE WAS KING OF THAT MOUNTAIN AND THAT GOD ALMIGHTY AND ALL THE REBELS OF HELL COULD NOT DRIVE HIM FROM IT."
—COLONEL ISAAC SHELBY, DESCRIBING MAJOR PATRICK FERGUSON

Some of the patriot leaders were veterans of Lord Dunmore's War in 1774 against the Shawnee and Mingo Indians and they had developed unconventional battle strategies as a result. At about 3 P.M. on the day of the battle, the patriots attacked in a four-column formation. Campbell led one of the interior columns. Their years of hunting in the mountains and fighting Indians paid off. They fired from behind trees and rocks, a style of warfare that flustered Ferguson and his troops. The patriots decimated their enemies and killed Ferguson.

The Tories tried to surrender to the patriots' leader, but they could not find him. Campbell had removed his coat and was fighting in an open-collared shirt. No one could single him out as the elected commander. Finally, the slaughter abated of its own accord.

FEDERAL FACTS

Allegedly, the patriots stripped Major Ferguson's clothes from his body and urinated on his remains before burying him near where he fell.

The Battle of Kings Mountain lasted about one hour. Casualty figures show how one sided it was. There were 225 Tories killed, 163 wounded, and 716 captured. Not one of them escaped! Only twenty-eight patriots were killed and sixty-eight wounded.

The unheralded—but historically significant—battle all but ended the war in the South.

The Final Promotion

After General Cornwallis heard about the outcome of the Battle of Kings Mountain, he withdrew his troops from North Carolina and assembled them near Winnsboro, South Carolina. But it was too late for him.

Within a few months the Continental Army and their militia counterparts chased Cornwallis out of South Carolina, the South in general, and the United States. Campbell had earned himself a place in history, but he did not live long enough to realize what he had accomplished.

The Virginia Assembly commissioned William Campbell as a brigadier general in 1781. It was his last promotion. In June of that year, Campbell joined the French military leader Marquis de Lafayette in eastern Virginia to continue the campaign against the British. On August 22, 1781, he suffered an apparent heart attack and died.

The assembly granted 5,000 acres of land to his young son, Charles Henry Campbell, to express its appreciation for his father's distinguished service.

The "Campbell created by a committee" had driven a lethal nail into the British army's campaign to defeat the American enemy. More importantly, he had shown that some of the biggest heroes in the war for independence were not Founding Fathers: They were often everyday Americans, whose numbers formed the biggest committee of patriots in the country.

SAMUEL CHASE

There was nothing in Samuel Chase's early life to suggest that he was destined to play a leading role in the American Revolution or its aftermath. He was homeschooled by his father, an Episcopalian clergyman, earned a law degree, and practiced law for several years. Chase engaged in activities as a member of the Sons of Liberty that might earn him a label of "terrorist" today. Nevertheless, he was elected to the Continental Congress, where he served on twenty-one committees in 1777 and thirty in 1778, convinced his fellow Marylanders to vote for independence, signed the Declaration of Independence, fell afoul of Alexander Hamilton when he tried to make a few dollars, became a Supreme Court justice, and was impeached. He was a sometimes controversial, but always well-meaning, patriot whose penchant for acting rashly at times separated him from most of his contemporaries.

An Innocuous Beginning

Chase got an early start in politics as a member of the Maryland General Assembly, where he served from 1764–1784.

Chase, an ardent proponent of independence as a young man, was not shy about letting people know where he stood on the issue. He did more than talk about his patriotism; he acted on it.

REVOLUTIONARY REVELATIONS

One of the proposed laws Chase supported in the Maryland General Assembly would have regulated the salaries of the colony's clergy. He believed the law would serve the people's best interests—even though it would have cut his Episcopal clergyman father's salary in half.

Chase was an active member of the Sons of Liberty, a group of American patriots who banded together in 1766 to protect the colonists from a growing number of onerous British laws. After the passage of the Stamp Act, he led a group of Sons in a raid on the Annapolis, Maryland, public offices, where they destroyed the tax stamps and burned the king's tax agent in effigy. He was twenty-four years old at the time.

Not surprisingly, Chase was not a popular young man among town officials in Annapolis. They preferred that he take his tendency for rebellion and insurrection elsewhere. In a classic "be careful what you wish for" case, he did. The leaders of the movement for independence wanted men like Chase on their side. In 1774, Chase and four other Maryland patriots were appointed delegates to the First Continental Congress.

Quotations to Live (and Die) By!

"[SAMUEL CHASE IS A] BUSY, RESTLESS INCENDIARY, A RINGLEADER OF MOBS, A FOUL-MOUTHED AND INFLAMING SON OF DISCORD AND FACTION, A COMMON DISTURBER OF THE PUBLIC TRANQUILITY, AND A PROMOTER OF THE LAWLESS EXCESSES OF THE MULTITUDE."

—ANNAPOLIS TOWN OFFICIALS

Cut to the Chase

Chase performed so well at the First Continental Congress that Maryland offered him the chance to return to the Second Continental Congress in 1775. When it came time to form a committee at that Congress, Chase was usually available. Due to his popularity and indefatigable nature, he remained a member of Congress until 1778.

When the members of the Second Continental Congress gathered to sign the Declaration of Independence, Chase was among them. It was a proud day for him, but signing the document did not curb his relentless pursuit of liberty or fairness for soldiers and citizens.

Amidst all his hard work Chase hit a bump in the road. In 1778, he and a group of individuals capitalized on some insider trading information. They cornered the market on flour in anticipation of making a huge sale to the French fleet coming to the aid of the United States. Alexander Hamilton exposed the scheme and wrote about it in New York newspapers under the pseudonym Publius. The affair did not attract a lot of attention, but Maryland left Chase out of its congressional delegation for the next two years, possibly in retribution for his involvement in the grain affair. He was reappointed in 1784, but stayed inactive in congressional proceedings after his return.

FEDERAL FACTS

One of Chase's early 1776 assignments was to work on a committee with Benjamin Franklin and fellow Marylander Charles Carroll of Carrollton, who used the "Carrollton" to distinguish himself from his father, Charles Carroll of Annapolis. Their assignment was to win the hearts and minds of Canadians. The trio visited Canada in an effort to convince the residents to side with the colonies in their attempt to separate from Britain. There was an ongoing—but unrelated—attempt by patriot militant forces to oust the British troops from Canada. That ended in June 1776, when British troops drove the Americans back to Fort Ticonderoga. In the end, the American army and the committee failed miserably.

In 1786, Chase moved to Baltimore, where he became chief judge of the criminal court and later chief judge of the General Court of Maryland. Those assignments paved the way for his appointment to the U.S. Supreme Court by President George Washington on January 26, 1796.

Chase served on the Supreme Court for fifteen years and became the first—and only—Supreme Court justice ever impeached. The impeachment happened when President Thomas Jefferson "suggested" to the House of Representatives in 1803 that it impeach Chase, ostensibly because he did not give John Fries, a defendant in a treason case, a fair trial. The real reason may have been Jefferson's desire to get rid of Chase because he did not agree with Jefferson's political views. The impeachment proceedings in 1805 became a politically motivated circus. Congress failed to get the two-thirds majority it needed to convict Chase.

FEDERAL FACTS

The Americans named a committee in January 1777 to investigate British atrocities at New York and New Jersey in late 1776, e.g., when they implemented martial law in Queens, New York, and their troops raped, robbed, and cheated the inhabitants. Chase was named as a member. In addition to participating in the investigation, he vigorously advocated for higher pay for the soldiers fighting the war, even if it required wage and price controls throughout the colonies to raise the money.

REVOLUTIONARY REVELATIONS

Chase campaigned against the U.S. Constitution for two reasons. He believed that the federal government's ability to tax citizens and regulate commerce would inhibit the states' rights to do the same, and he did not see any protection in the Constitution for individuals' rights. Chase saw the proposed Constitution as a reversion to British rule—which he had spent a good part of his life fighting to throw off.

The impeachment and severe attacks of gout had an adverse effect on Chase. He lost some of his fire after 1805, but it had burned brightly up until that point—enough to fuel the flame of liberty for the crucial years during the struggle for American independence. Chase had gone from incendiary to being impugned and impeached in his lifetime, but he exemplified the resiliency of the men and women who established American independence.

HENRY CLAY

Hanover County, Virginia
April 12, 1777–June 29, 1852
The Bridge

Henry Clay, an active politician in the first half of the nineteenth century, was one of the people who supported and maintained what the Founding Fathers had built. He moved to Kentucky five years after it became the country's fifteenth state in 1792, and served as a state representative, U.S. congressman and senator, governor of Kentucky, and United States secretary of state. The experiences he gained in these positions molded Clay into an astute politician capable of dealing with national problems such as the implementation of a new economic system and the slavery issue. Clay was a throwback to the original Founding Fathers. He bridged the gap between the infant and adolescent United States and influenced a new style of political leadership that introduced innovative policies that steered the country into its adult phase. He was a perfect example of the right man in the right place at the right time—for a long time—just as the Founding Fathers had been.

Political Ping-Pong

Henry Clay was elected to the Kentucky state House of Representatives in 1803. Three years later, he was appointed to the U.S. Senate—in violation of the U.S. Constitution, which mandated that senators had to be at least thirty years old. He was twenty-nine years old when he took office.

Clay's stay in the Senate was short. His appointment lasted from November 19, 1806, to March 3, 1807—and he was still not yet thirty when he stepped down.

REVOLUTIONARY REVELATIONS

Henry Clay defended Aaron Burr in 1806 on charges that he was conspiring to separate the western states from the rest of the country. Burr beat the rap. Thomas Jefferson persuaded Clay later that Burr had been guilty. The victory in court turned into a bitter defeat for Clay. When he bumped into Burr in New York nine years later, Clay refused to shake his former client's hand.

Clay returned to the state assembly for the 1808–09 session, becoming Speaker of the Kentucky House of Representatives. After Humphrey Marshall objected to Clay's motion to require members of the Assembly to wear homespun suits instead of British clothing, the two engaged in fisticuffs on the House floor. That led to a three-round duel in which Clay inflicted a slight flesh wound on Marshall's side during the first round of shots. Both men missed their shots in the second round. In the third and final round, Marshall shot Clay in the thigh. That ended the duel.

 Quotations to Live (and Die) By!

"GOVERNMENT IS A TRUST, AND THE OFFICERS OF THE GOVERNMENT ARE TRUSTEES; AND BOTH THE TRUST AND THE TRUSTEES ARE CREATED FOR THE BENEFIT OF THE PEOPLE."
—HENRY CLAY

Then, it was back to the U.S. Senate in Washington, D.C. to replace Buckner Thruston, whom President James Madison had appointed to a judge's seat on the United States Circuit Court of the District of Columbia. Clay was of legal age this time.

The Revolving Door Keeps Spinning

After completing his second short term as a U.S. Senator, Clay returned to the U.S. House of Representatives until President James Monroe appointed him as one of the commissioners charged with negotiating a peace treaty with Britain to end the War of 1812. And on it went. For the next thirty-seven years Clay made his presence known in every major event in the nation's evolution.

REVOLUTIONARY REVELATIONS

Henry Clay once filled his own vacant congressional seat. The governor of Kentucky declared Clay's seat vacant so he could accept a position as envoy to Britain. Once he completed the assignment, he won a special election in 1815 to fill his own vacant seat.

Clay encouraged the United States to go to war with Britain in 1812 to end once and for all the indignities he felt Britain had been inflicting on the United States since 1805, such as the seizure of American merchant vessels and the impressments of their crews.

Clay advocated tariffs on imported goods to help bolster the country's economy as part of "The American System," a program he designed to balance the roles of agriculture, commerce, and industry in the nation's economy. He refereed the Missouri Compromise to settle the slavery impasse, working out an agreement where new states except Missouri above a fixed line between the north and south would be slave free, while those beneath it could retain their slaves. Thus, he contained the spread of slavery, although it remained legal in some states. The compromise was Clay's signature achievement, although it turned out to be far from a permanent solution to the slavery problem in the United States. Based on his achievements and negotiating skills, Clay was among the first statesmen people turned to when they sought settlements in thorny issues.

Quotations to Live (and Die) By!

"SHOULD ANY OF OUR VESSELS BE HEREAFTER SEIZED AND CONDEMNED, HOWEVER UNJUSTLY, AND THAT ALL WILL BE SEIZED AND CONDEMNED MAY BE CONFIDENTLY EXPECTED, WE MUST BE SILENT, OR BE HEARD BY FOREIGN POWERS IN THE HUMBLE LANGUAGE OF PETITION ONLY."

—HENRY CLAY IN A LETTER IN SUPPORT OF THE WAR OF 1812

The "Corrupt Bargain"

Clay was not always appreciated by his fellow politicians. One of the low points of his career occurred in 1824, when he ran for president of the United States.

The 1824 presidential election was one of the most confusing campaigns in American history. Four members of the Democratic-Republican party vied for the presidency. They included Clay, Andrew Jackson, John Quincy Adams, and William Crawford. None of them earned the victory after the election results were tallied.

Clay finished fourth in the popular and Electoral College voting. He won 13.1 percent of the popular vote and 37 of the 261 electoral votes. Jackson and Adams had the highest number of electoral votes. Clay believed that Adams was more amenable to his policies and would be more helpful to him than Jackson as president—and might even appoint him to his cabinet. He used his influence to sway the House of Representatives, which would settle the issue, to elect Adams. It did, and Clay got his coveted cabinet position.

Adams appointed Clay as secretary of state. He served in that position from 1825–29. Jackson and his followers declared Clay's action as a "corrupt bargain." Clay did not see what he did as corruption; it was politics as usual.

Despite the stain on his reputation, he exercised his influence for the rest of his career, which ultimately spanned half a century. His list of accomplishments was significant throughout that time. He was still serving in the U.S. Senate when he died, well over the legally mandated minimum age.

LYDIA DARRAGH

Dublin, Ireland
1728–December 28, 1789
A Mother's Instinct

Lydia Darragh, a Quaker and resident of Philadelphia, helped save Washington's army from defeat at White Marsh, Pennsylvania, in December 1777. She did it by using a sack of flour as a pretext and making a dangerous trek outside the city to warn the Americans that General William Howe was heading their way. Afterwards, she returned to the mundane life she was used to—and excommunication by the Quakers.

A Victim of the Quartering Acts Mentality

When the British occupied Philadelphia on September 26, 1777, the Darraghs were told to vacate their dwelling as the Quartering Acts allowed the British to demand.

Lydia Darragh asked General Howe, who was domiciled nearby, if she could stay in her home. She explained that she had already sent her two youngest children to live with relatives and that she had no place else to go.

Howe offered a compromise. If she would reserve a room in her house where British officers could hold meetings, she could stay, as long as she gave them complete privacy.

Done, said Darragh. Unknowingly, Howe had made a tactical blunder.

Lydia Darragh Becomes a Snoop

There were no discernible problems with Darragh's living arrangements at first. On December 2, 1777, several British officers, including Howe, showed up at the house for a meeting. They warned Darragh to make sure nobody lingered around the meeting room. Howe's purpose for the meeting was twofold: to discuss new information he had acquired from his spies regarding Washington's move to a new camp and to plan how to catch the Americans in the open, when they were most vulnerable.

Darragh suspected the British were up to devilry, and that their plans might have a bearing on her son Charles, who was fighting with the Second Pennsylvania Regiment stationed near White Marsh. Darragh's maternal instincts prompted her to turn a linen closet next to the meeting room into a listening post. What she heard through the wall confirmed her suspicions. Howe was planning to attack Washington near White Marsh, thirteen miles down the road.

She improvised a plan to thwart the British.

A Flour Sack and a Brisk Hike

Darragh decided on a way to warn Washington. All she needed was a pass and a flour sack. Local citizens often asked British authorities for passes to places outside the city where they could buy supplies. The British routinely authorized the requests. Accordingly, Darragh procured a pass to the flour mill in nearby Frankford.

With flour sack in hand, she headed through the snow in that direction. She also had with her a notebook in which she kept notes about the information she garnered in Philadelphia. She reached the mill—and kept right on going.

According to the diary of Colonel Elias Boudinot, Washington's commissary general of prisoners, she handed her notebook to him as he was dining at the Rising Sun Tavern, north of the city, along the route to White Marsh. Boudinot passed the information to Washington.

"Did You Do It?"

The British marched out of Philadelphia on December 4 to surprise Washington. But Washington was ready for them. Based on the information Darragh had fed Boudinot, Washington knew Howe's strength. According to Boudinot, Darragh had given him "a piece of paper rolled up into the form of a pipe shank. On unrolling it I found information that General Howe was coming out the next morning with 5,000 men, 13 pieces of cannon, baggage wagons, and 11 boat on wheels. On comparing this with other information, I found it true and immediately rode post to headquarters."

The two armies sparred around the area for the next few days. Neither gained an advantage, and damages were held to a minimum.

FEDERAL FACTS
There were 150 Americans killed or wounded and fifty-four captured at White Marsh. The British suffered 112 casualties, seventy-nine of whom were killed or wounded. The more significant statistic for the British was the number of missing (thirty-three) and desertions—a staggering 238 soldiers.

Howe returned to Philadelphia, convinced that he could not destroy Washington's army. That ended the fighting in 1777. Six months later the British left Philadelphia and the reunited Darragh family moved back into their house on Second Street—but not before Lydia misled the British for the last time.

The day after the British troops returned to Philadelphia, British Major John André visited Darragh's house and asked her if she had tipped off the Americans about Howe's plans. She said no. André was not convinced, but he let the matter drop. Unfortunately, the Quakers did not.

Quotations to Live (and Die) By!

"ONE THING IS CERTAIN. THE ENEMY HAD NOTICE
OF OUR COMING, WERE PREPARED FOR US, AND WE
MARCHED BACK LIKE A PARCEL OF FOOLS. THE WALLS
MUST HAVE EARS."

—JOHN ANDRÉ TO LYDIA DARRAGH ON DECEMBER 9, 1777

Technically, Darragh could have been treated as a traitor and executed had the British determined that she was a spy, but they didn't. However, the Quakers excommunicated her in 1783—the same year her husband died—because of her involvement in the war. They reinstated her in 1789—the same year she died.

After the war, Darragh operated a store in Philadelphia, the city that owed her so much for her heroic stand that saved it from possible permanent occupation—and Washington from a devastating military defeat.

FEDERAL FACTS

Darragh was one of the many "not your father's founders" who were willing to set aside their Quaker beliefs temporarily in support of war. Others included John Dickinson, Joseph Hewes, and Patrick Henry.

SILAS DEANE

Groton, Connecticut
December 24, 1737–September 23, 1789
Framed Framer

Silas Deane was just the man the Americans needed to convince the French to support their cause. He was a wealthy lawyer, merchant, and politician whose diplomatic skills were supposed to complement those of his fellow ambassadors, Benjamin Franklin and Arthur Lee, although it did not turn out that way. But he was also willing to use the war as an opportunity to make a profit for himself, which didn't always sit well with some patriots—and led to questions in Congress about his integrity and judgment. Deane, a member of the Connecticut Colonial Assembly (1772–74) and the Continental Congress from 1774–76, persuaded a few European military officers to enlist in the Continental armed forces to fight against the British. Some of the European officers were more interested in personal glory than the American cause. For his efforts, Deane was recalled under a cloud of suspicion, exiled from his home country, and possibly murdered.

From Connecticut to France

Silas Deane was solidifying his reputation in Connecticut as a man to be trusted in the days leading up to the American Revolution based on his integrity as a businessman and representative in the colony's General Assembly. When the call went out for delegates to the First Continental Congress in 1774, Deane was among those chosen, and he was reappointed in 1775.

Deane was optimistic that the Congress could find a way to get the colonies out from under British rule. He was even more convinced after he arrived in the thriving city of Philadelphia, the largest city in the colonies at the time, and met the other delegates of distinction. Congressional leaders were so impressed with his abilities that they sent him to France to seek French support for American independence.

Deane joined Franklin and Lee in Paris to negotiate an alliance with France. The United States and France signed two separate treaties on February 6, 1778: the Treaty of Alliance, and a Treaty of Amity and Commerce that promoted trade and commercial ties between the two countries. According to the terms of the Treaty of Alliance, both countries agreed not to negotiate a separate peace with Great Britain. More importantly, American independence would be a condition of any future peace agreement.

REVOLUTIONARY REVELATIONS

Silas Deane and his brother Simeon operated a successful privateering business during the war. They, like so many other merchant-patriots, were adept at converting patriotism into profits in the interest of helping their country.

"Jealous-Lee"

The arms and supplies France sent to the Continental Army played a major role in its surprising victory over British troops at Saratoga, New York, in September and October 1777. Historians suggest that the victory was the turning point in the war. It elevated the Continental Army's morale and removed the aura of invincibility many Americans thought surrounded their British foe.

But Arthur Lee grew jealous of Silas Deane's success in Paris and accused Deane that year of embezzling some of the funds intended to pay for such arms. Lee suspected Franklin had done the same thing, which Franklin denied.

Congress recalled Deane to investigate his alleged questionable conduct. On November 27, 1777, it appointed John Adams to replace Deane in Paris.

Deane delayed his return to the colonies until the treaties were signed. Then he returned in a triumphant manner aboard a French warship to defend himself. It was not surprising that Deane made a few business deals of his own in Paris. After all, he arrived there in July 1776 ostensibly as a businessman. The Committee of Secret Correspondence had told him, "On your arrival in France, you will for some time be engaged in the business of providing goods for the Indian trade. This will give good countenance to your appearing in the character of a merchant, which we wish you continually to retain among the French, in general, it being probable that the court of France may not like it should be known publicly that any agent from the Colonies is in that country."

Nothing More Than Shoddy Bookkeeping

Perhaps Deane created some of his troubles. Several of the European officers he recruited comported themselves badly during the war. Irish General Thomas Conway became involved in a cabal to overthrow General George Washington, and Comte de Broglie, the Marquis de Lafayette, and Baron de Kalb hatched a scheme to install Lafayette as the commander in chief of the American army. Critics viewed Deane's involvement with such officers as a reflection on his inability to assess officers' ethics and leadership skills. And there was no doubt Deane and some silent partners were making lucrative business deals on the side. There were no direct connections between and among the various charges and suspicions about Deane's conduct in Paris, but Congress was determined to investigate Lee's allegations.

The long, bitter hearings regarding Deane's conduct were messy. France refused to furnish copies of receipts and other documents, claiming that to do so would demonstrate that they had been involved in diplomatic negotiations with a noncountry prior to signing treaties with it. That would embarrass the French.

Deane went on the offensive. He demanded that Congress break off diplomatic relations with France and questioned the integrity of members of Congress who disagreed with him.

Deane returned to Paris in 1781 to find copies of documents such as receipts and journal entries that would prove his innocence. But, Congress was in no hurry to review the accounts he prepared. His cause was lost. Worse, his American colleagues were reluctant to let him return to the colonies because they thought he was a traitor to their cause.

A Man Without a Country

Deane stayed in Europe for a few years, first in the Netherlands and then England, where he lived in poverty. He published a defense of his actions in *An Address to the Free and Independent Citizens of the United States of North America*, which was published in Hartford, Connecticut, and London in 1784. He planned a return to the United States in 1789 to establish his innocence and reclaim his wealth, but he became mysteriously ill before his ship sailed for home. There was some speculation that he had been poisoned deliberately by a British spy. He died on September 23, 1789.

Congress never found Deane guilty of anything. His family did not believe he was. His granddaughter Philura and her husband pressed Congress to review his case. It did—and exonerated him.

Deane was one of the most ill-fated of the founders of the United States. At least he has a highway, a school, and a library named after him in Wethersfield, Connecticut. Someone believed in him—albeit many years after he died in disgrace.

FEDERAL FACTS

Silas Deane's family received $37,000 in 1841 after Congress determined that a former audit was "ex parte (from a one-sided or strongly biased point of view), erroneous, and a gross injustice to Silas Deane."

JOHN DICKINSON

Talbot County, Maryland
November 20, 1732–February 14, 1808
An Enigma Wrapped in a Puzzle

The highly principled John Dickinson offered incontrovertible proof that not all the Founding Fathers always saw eye to eye. He was at various times a Continental Congressman from Pennsylvania and Delaware, president of both colonies/states, a delegate to the U.S. Constitutional Convention of 1787, a successful lawyer, and one of the wealthiest men in America. He was also one of the most enigmatic Founding Fathers, singled out by a unique legacy: He had a new college in Carlisle, Pennsylvania named after him, twenty-five years *before* he died.

Law School and Leadership

Dickinson began studying law in his adopted city, Philadelphia, when he was eighteen years old. Five years later he moved to London to continue his studies. He gained an affinity for the British Constitution while he was there, which affected his thinking when he returned to the colonies. Dickinson believed that the colonists should adhere to its tenets. He argued that their gripes were with the British Parliament, not its constitution, and could be resolved according to constitutional principles.

After he returned to the colonies, Dickinson married into a Quaker family. His family had Quaker roots, but had disassociated itself from the society after his sister, Betsy, was married in an Anglican church. The

Quakers labeled her marriage as a "disorderly marriage," which displeased John and Betsy's father, who broke off relations with the society.

REVOLUTIONARY REVELATIONS

Unlike many of his contemporaries and colleagues, Dickinson did not sign the Declaration of Independence. He was adamantly opposed to American independence and believed firmly that the colonies and Britain could reconcile if only the patriots would cool their rhetoric. He recommended that the colonies form a confederation before declaring independence.

Quotations to Live (and Die) By!

"KINGS OR PARLIAMENTS COULD NOT GIVE THE RIGHTS ESSENTIAL TO HAPPINESS. . . . WE CLAIM THEM FROM A HIGHER SOURCE—FROM THE KING OF KINGS, AND LORD OF ALL THE EARTH. THEY ARE NOT ANNEXED TO US BY PARCHMENTS AND SEALS. THEY ARE CREATED IN US BY THE DECREES OF PROVIDENCE, WHICH ESTABLISH THE LAWS OF OUR NATURE. THEY ARE BORN WITH US; EXIST WITH US; AND CANNOT BE TAKEN FROM US BY ANY HUMAN POWER, WITHOUT TAKING OUR LIVES."

—JOHN DICKINSON

Nevertheless, John married Mary ("Polly") Norris on July 19, 1770. Her father, Isaac, was the Speaker of the Pennsylvania General Assembly and one of the wealthiest men in the colony. The marriage increased his access to wealth and political prowess due to the Norris family's influence, but it did not lead him to become an active Quaker, although he retained a belief in the society's principles. Dickinson had no objections to defensive war, in contrast to the pacifistic views held by the Norris family.

Dickinson's political career blossomed in the mid-1770s and early 1780s. He became a First Continental Congressman from Pennsylvania effective August 2, 1774, which positioned him to participate in the discussions about independence in 1776. As a member of the First and Second Continental Congresses, he was well versed in what the colonists wanted. He did not necessarily want what most of them did.

Dickinson the Contrarian

Dickinson did not advocate independence or revolution. He favored reconciliation. Nevertheless, he worked closely with other delegates to promote the colonists' search for a solution to the "British problem." He and Thomas Jefferson collaborated on *A Declaration of the Causes and Necessity of Taking Up Arms*, which received considerable attention. In that declaration, Dickinson concluded that Americans were "resolved to die free men rather than live slaves."

Despite his close relationships with the Philadelphia delegates in 1776, Dickinson continued to urge for a peaceful agreement with Britain. He had made clear his stance regarding independence, taxes, and other issues regarding British-American relations in his well-known tract, *Letters from a Farmer in Pennsylvania*, which comprised a series of essays he wrote under an assumed name in 1767–68. In them, he argued that the colonies were sovereign in their internal affairs and that taxes levied by Parliament to raise revenues instead of regulating trade were unconstitutional.

Dickinson's letters circulated widely among the thirteen colonies and laid the groundwork for the arguments against many of the revenue-generating laws imposed by Parliament. They earned him the title of "Penman of the Revolution." He stayed true to his principles.

I'll Join the Army Instead

Dickinson tried to convince his counterparts that independence was not in their best interests. They argued otherwise. At the vote for independence on July 2, 1776, he abstained. Nor did he cast a ballot on July 4 when Congress voted on the wording on the formal declaration. Dickinson believed he had one choice after independence won the day: leave the meeting. He did so with a heavy heart and misgivings about his personal and political future.

Quotations to Live (and Die) By!

"My conduct this day, I expect will give the finishing blow to my once too great and, my integrity considered, now too diminished popularity."
—John Dickinson after the July 4, 1776, vote

After the Congress adjourned, Dickinson accepted an assignment as a brigadier general in the Pennsylvania militia. He led 10,000 troops to Elizabeth, New Jersey, to help protect the area from an anticipated British invasion. But when two junior officers were promoted above him, probably due to his unpopular stance against independence, he resigned his commission and returned to his estate in Delaware.

Like so many other patriots, Dickinson paid a material price for his resistance to Britain. Even though Dickinson was not 100 percent committed to independence, the British did not do him any favors during the war. They confiscated his mansion in Philadelphia while he was in Delaware and turned it into a hospital. They burned his wife's family's estate, Fairhill, during the Battle of Germantown in Pennsylvania on October 4, 1777. To make matters worse, Tories ransacked another of his residences, Poplar Hill, in August 1781.

The End Was Not Near

Despite Dickinson's unhappy departure from the Second Continental Congress, he retained his popularity among voters. After the war he held several political offices, including those of president of Delaware and president of Pennsylvania, at the same time.

Dickinson left active politics in 1793 after a final term in the Delaware Senate. He spent the next fifteen years working to advance the abolition of slavery and writing his collected works on politics, which he published in 1801. Dickinson also donated a significant portion of his wealth to the "relief of the unhappy." His benevolence became a part of his strange legacy—and his death did not go unnoticed among his former colleagues.

FEDERAL FACTS

It was legal for individuals to hold offices in two states in the late eighteenth century if the officeholder owned property in both.

Quotations to Live (and Die) By!

"A MORE ESTIMABLE MAN, OR TRUER PATRIOT, COULD NOT HAVE LEFT US. AMONG THE FIRST OF THE ADVOCATES FOR THE RIGHTS OF HIS COUNTRY WHEN ASSAILED BY GREAT BRITAIN, HE CONTINUED TO THE LAST THE ORTHODOX ADVOCATE OF THE TRUE PRINCIPLES OF OUR NEW GOVERNMENT AND HIS NAME WILL BE CONSECRATED IN HISTORY AS ONE OF THE GREAT WORTHIES OF THE REVOLUTION."

—THOMAS JEFFERSON

Despite his unwillingness to vote for independence in 1776, John Dickinson never lost the respect of his fellow patriots, although he perplexed them because of his principled stances on issues and his insistence on making his views known in plain terms. Nothing Dickinson did or said should have surprised them.

REVOLUTIONARY REVELATIONS

John Dickinson believed that it was not always necessary for him to do what people—even those who elected him—expected. It was more important to do what he considered right.

Because he was such an enigma, John Dickinson is often overlooked by historians regarding his role in the movement for independence.

BENJAMIN FRANKLIN

Boston, Massachusetts
January 17, 1706–April 17, 1790
20,000 Accomplishments

Apprentice . . . writer . . . runaway . . . workaholic . . . printer . . . entrepreneur . . . lover . . . cartoonist . . . activist . . . firefighter . . . inventor . . . politician . . . agitator . . . spy . . . signer . . . ambassador . . . Francophile . . . diplomat . . . delegate . . . Those are only a few of the words that describe Benjamin Franklin. He was unique among Americans. At various times he was the colonial agent for Georgia, New Jersey, and Massachusetts; a delegate from Pennsylvania to the Continental Congress; a signer of the Declaration of Independence; a commissioner of Congress to the French court; a negotiator and a signer of the Treaty of Paris that ended the Revolutionary War; an inventor; and a businessman. His eclecticism set him apart from his contemporaries and made him truly unique among the people who established the United States.

A Man for All Reasons

Even though Benjamin Franklin's early education was limited, he was reading authors like Plutarch, Daniel Defoe, and Cotton Mather by the time he was eleven—which was the age at which he invented a pair of swim fins for his hands. Early signs suggested that Benjamin Franklin would be different from most boys his age. He was.

Quotations to Live (and Die) By!

"THE ESSENCE OF THE WHOLE WILL BE THAT DR. FRANKLIN'S ELECTRICAL ROD SMOTE THE EARTH AND OUT SPRUNG GENERAL WASHINGTON. THAT FRANKLIN ELECTRIFIED HIM WITH HIS ROD AND THENCE FORWARD THESE TWO CONDUCTED ALL THE POLICY, NEGOTIATION, LEGISLATION, AND WAR."

—JOHN ADAMS

When he was twelve years old, Benjamin apprenticed as a printer in the shop owned by his mean-spirited and physically abusive older brother James. James, who became responsible for Benjamin's upbringing, beat him physically on occasion. And he would not let Benjamin write for his new paper, the *New England Courant*, that James founded in 1721. Tired of the mental and physical abuse, Benjamin ran away at age seventeen and ended up in Philadelphia. Since printing was all Benjamin knew, he took up the trade.

REVOLUTIONARY REVELATIONS

Benjamin craftily got around James's ban on his writing. He wrote advice letters under the name of Silence Dogood, a fictional widow, which James printed. Benjamin pushed the letters under the door of the office at night and pretended he did not know who the writer was. He wrote sixteen letters under Dogood's name before he admitted that he was she. James was not happy.

Social Engineering in Philadelphia

Franklin's career took off in Philadelphia. He wrote a number of pamphlets, started his own business, and, in 1727, established the Junto, a society of young men that met on Friday evenings for "self-improvement, study, mutual aid, and conviviality." The group contributed greatly to his educational and social development. In between, he sired a son, William, out of wedlock.

REVOLUTIONARY REVELATIONS

Benjamin Franklin became a vegetarian in 1722, mainly because he wanted to use the money saved from not buying meat to purchase books.

Over the next few years Franklin was the creator of or advisor to a number of social organizations aimed at improving life in Philadelphia, including a fire department, a library, and an insurance company. His most notable achievement may have been the launching of *Poor Richard's Almanack* under the name of Richard Saunders, which was full of pithy sayings that are repeated today: "A penny saved is a penny earned," "Without justice, courage is weak," and "In success be moderate."

Running a business and improving society were not satisfying enough for Franklin. He began dabbling in science and experimentation as well. In 1743, he invented the Franklin stove, a heat-efficient stove that made heating houses easier and less costly. Since it improved society, he refused to take out a patent. In 1752, he flew a kite in his famous experiment that demonstrated lightning was made of electricity.

REVOLUTIONARY REVELATIONS

Benjamin's son William became the royal governor of New Jersey in 1763. He remained loyal to Britain throughout his tenure, which ended in 1776. The political differences between the two created a rift that they never resolved. It was heartbreaking for Benjamin, especially after William moved to England permanently in 1782.

All his activities drew the attention of his adoring public, and led him into politics. He was as proficient at that as he was in virtually everything else he tried.

Ben the Politician

Although Franklin was not convinced early in his life that the colonies should be free of British rule, he changed his mind as the 1760s progressed.

He lived in London as an agent for several colonies, including Georgia, Massachusetts, and New Jersey. He grew to dislike the way the British people viewed the colonists. As Franklin wrote, "Every man in England seems to consider himself as a piece of a sovereign over America."

He had an opportunity to oppose the British government in 1775, when he was elected as a delegate from Pennsylvania to the Second Continental Congress. The next year he helped draft the Declaration of Independence, and then signed it.

 Quotations to Live (and Die) By!

"THEY WHO CAN GIVE UP ESSENTIAL LIBERTY TO OBTAIN A LITTLE TEMPORARY SAFETY DESERVE NEITHER LIBERTY NOR SAFETY."

—BENJAMIN FRANKLIN

No one expected Franklin to serve actively in the military during the Revolutionary War. After all, he was sixty-six years old when he signed the Declaration of Independence. Instead, he was dispatched overseas to seek French assistance with America's war effort. He arrived in Paris on December 21, 1776, as one of the members of the commissioners of Congress to the French court. He did not return until 1785.

Franklin negotiated successfully with the French for aid to the United States. Then, between 1779 and 1781 he was appointed to a commission to negotiate a peace treaty with Britain. He signed the Treaty of Alliance with the French government in 1778 and the peace treaty ending the Revolutionary War in 1783.

REVOLUTIONARY REVELATIONS

Two of Franklin's cleverest inventions were created in the 1783–86 period: bifocals and a device for pulling books off shelves.

One More Major Assignment

After Franklin returned to the United States, he kept busy. He served as president of the Pennsylvania Executive Council, which was the executive branch of the state's government, from 1785 to 1788.

In 1787, he served as a delegate to the Philadelphia Convention to debate the merits of the U.S. Constitution, but he did not participate often in the discussions. Nevertheless, he signed the document after it was ratified.

Quotations to Live (and Die) By!

"IF YOU WOULD NOT BE FORGOTTEN, AS SOON AS YOU ARE DEAD AND ROTTEN, EITHER WRITE THINGS WORTHY READING, OR DO THINGS WORTH THE WRITING."
—BENJAMIN FRANKLIN

He concentrated on the abolition of slavery for the next couple of years. But time caught up with him in 1790. He passed away at age eighty-four. About 20,000 people attended his funeral—seemingly one for every accomplishment in his extremely productive lifetime.

Elbridge Gerry seemingly came out of nowhere, signed the Declaration of Independence, and returned to obscurity, except for the word for which he is still remembered: "Gerrymandering." Before he bequeathed the country with that eponym, he served in several legislative bodies and as an envoy to France. He lost a little cachet when he refused to vote for the U.S. Constitution, but he rebounded to become the governor of Massachusetts and the vice president of the United States. Those were significant accomplishments for a man with obscure beginnings.

Who Was Elbridge Gerry?

If Elbridge Gerry had not signed the Declaration of Independence, his epitaph might have been short: "He was born in Massachusetts, graduated from Harvard, served his state well, and died in office." But the people of Massachusetts saw him as an effective legislator who deserved to take his place on the national stage. He did, without making much of a splash—except in a negative way.

Very little is known about Gerry's early life. He graduated from Harvard in 1762, became a wealthy merchant, and stumbled into politics.

In 1773, Gerry took a seat with the Massachusetts General Court to represent Marblehead. The following year Samuel Adams successfully introduced a motion asking that the province appoint a Committee of Correspondence and Inquiry. Gerry was named to the committee and participated enthusiastically, although he was not always happy with the way his fellow patriots acted in the name of liberty.

After the Boston Tea Party occurred—of which he strongly disapproved—Gerry took a break from politics. The British brought him out of his temporary hiatus when they closed the Boston port in 1774. Samuel Adams convinced Gerry that he had to do something about it.

It was all or nothing for Gerry. He became a member of the Committee of Safety, helped lead the colonists' armed response to the British, collected supplies, and recruited troops using his own money.

REVOLUTIONARY REVELATIONS

When the British marched on Lexington and Concord in April 1775, Gerry was staying at an inn along the route in Arlington. He did not take any chances as British troops approached the inn on the night of April 18, 1775. He escaped from possible detention by fleeing—still wearing his nightclothes.

As Active As Any Soldier

It was a second thought on the part of the citizens of Massachusetts, but they elected Gerry to the Second Continental Congress. Originally, Thomas Cushing was one of the colony's representatives to the Congress. But he refused to support independence. The citizens of Massachusetts did not see any sense in sending a delegate who would be counterproductive, so they elected Elbridge Gerry to replace Cushing. He rewarded their faith in him.

Gerry listened to arguments on both sides, and finally voted for independence, buoyed by his friends' pleas.

Quotations to Live (and Die) By!

"FOR GOD'S SAKE LET THERE BE A FULL REVOLUTION, OR
ALL HAS BEEN DONE IN VAIN."

—JOSEPH HAWLEY IN A MAY 1, 1776, LETTER TO ELBRIDGE GERRY

But he was absent on August 2, 1776, when the delegates signed the Declaration of Independence. He signed it on November 19, 1776, after he returned to Philadelphia.

Gerry stayed in Congress for several years after the war began. He served on a multitude of committees, and was active on the army's behalf.

Among other things, he helped design a general hospital for the army to replace regimental hospitals, which he considered impractical since they were difficult to move when a regiment relocated. Gerry also developed plans for instilling stricter discipline into the army and regulating the commissary's departments. He often visited army facilities to assess their financial statuses and make sure the military was paying its bills. After the war, he served another two-year term with the Continental Congress, then eased off on his activities until duty called once more.

Constitutionally Unacceptable

Gerry was selected as a delegate to the Constitutional Convention of 1787, even though he had reservations about the document. Faithful to his principles, he refused to sign it. He explained simply to his constituents that it had too many flaws. That didn't stop them from electing him to the U.S. House of Representatives in 1789, where he served two terms upholding the same document he had refused to sign.

After those two terms, Gerry declined to run for reelection. He tried to retire, but in 1797 President John Adams asked him to serve as an envoy with John Marshall and Charles Cotesworth Pinckney to France to try to resolve differences between the two countries regarding commerce. France sent Marshall and Pinckney home. Gerry stayed and helped reduce the tensions between the countries—temporarily, at least. After returning from France in October 1798, Gerry settled once again into retirement, which was as short-lived as his previous attempts.

Quotations to Live (and Die) By!

"MY PRINCIPAL OBJECTIONS TO THE PLAN ARE, THAT THERE IS NO ADEQUATE PROVISION FOR A REPRESENTATION OF THE PEOPLE; THAT THEY HAVE NO SECURITY FOR THE RIGHT OF ELECTION; THAT SOME OF THE POWERS OF THE LEGISLATURE ARE AMBIGUOUS, AND OTHERS INDEFINITE AND DANGEROUS . . ."

—A PARTIAL LIST OF ELBRIDGE GERRY'S OBJECTIONS TO THE U.S. CONSTITUTION

Gerry ran unsuccessfully for governor of Massachusetts in 1800, 1801, 1802, and 1803. He finally won the office in 1810. He served two terms as governor of Massachusetts. In 1812 the Massachusetts legislature redrew the boundaries of state legislative districts to favor Gerry's party. The word "gerrymandering" was coined to describe the process. It is used today in the same context. The process cost Gerry his reelection bid in 1812. That year, he began a partial term as vice president of the United States. He replaced

FEDERAL FACTS

The United States and France fought one another in the Quasi-War between 1798–1800 over treaty disputes, neutrality issues regarding the French Revolution, and French privateers' practices of preying on American merchant vessels. The war, fought entirely at sea, was a tactical win for the United States. The countries resolved it with the Treaty of Mortefontaine, signed on September 30, 1800.

George Clinton, who died in office on April 20, 1812. Strangely enough, Gerry did the same thing two-and-a-half years later.

He is not remembered for many of his other accomplishments, but he will always be known for "gerrymandering." That is his legacy.

NATHANAEL GREENE

Warwick, Rhode Island
August 7, 1742–June 19, 1786
You Don't Need to Win a Battle to Win a War

If there was a military science book available in Coventry, Rhode Island, in the 1750s, Nathanael Greene read it. The fact that he gained most of his military training through books rather than practical experience set him apart from most other military leaders in the Revolutionary War. However he acquired it, his military knowledge paid off later when he became one of George Washington's most trusted generals, capping a meteoric rise for the former member of the Rhode Island General Assembly and militiaman in a local company called the Kentish Guards.

On-the-Job Training

Greene was one of four Rhode Islanders to rush to Boston to offer his services after the battles at Lexington and Concord in April 1775. Shortly thereafter, the Rhode Island General Assembly authorized a force of 1,600 troops to travel to Massachusetts and appointed Greene to lead them. The Assembly was taking a chance. Greene's military experience to that point amounted to what he had learned from books in his large personal library and a bit of training with the Kentish Guards. That proved to be enough.

When Washington arrived in Boston to take command of the American troops, he and Greene bonded immediately. Their friendship and close working relationship contributed significantly to the Americans' ultimate military victory.

Washington and Greene took their war on the road and fought wherever they were needed following the successful conclusion to the siege of Boston. Where Washington went, Greene was sure to follow.

REVOLUTIONARY REVELATIONS

Greene had a unique perspective on serving his country as a soldier. Early in the war many patriots were willing to serve in their local areas. Once the army moved to a different locale they went home. Greene was not among them. He theorized that patriots' unwillingness to travel with the army would prevent a military victory.

Next Stop, New York

In 1776, Greene led troops during the battles at Long Island, New York City, and Princeton, New Jersey. On July 1, 1776, his troops were under great pressure on Long Island where British army units were massing to drive them away. Washington dispatched 500 men to reinforce him. Unfortunately, Greene became ill and missed the rest of the battle. He recovered in time to suffer severe anguish over the loss of Fort Washington in the Battle of New York.

There were better days ahead for him, but not always on the

FEDERAL FACTS

The Americans were desperate for supplies in 1776. In typical "good news, bad news" fashion, while Greene was calling for reinforcements, Washington's aide-de-camp, Samuel Blachley Webb, noted in his diary: "We have also received intelligence that our cruisers on the back of Long Island have taken and carried in one of the enemie's [sic] fleet laden with intrenching [sic] tools." At least Greene and his reinforcements could dig in for the battle, even if they had no hopes of winning it.

battlefield. Before his next major assignment after the defeat at New York, and a largely unsuccessful year on the battlefields in 1777, Greene had to help save Washington's job. A cabal of politicians and jealous officers formed a plot in late 1777 aimed at replacing Washington as commander in chief and ousting Greene because of his loyalty to the general. The loosely organized plot never came to fruition, due in part to Greene's refusal to support any attempts to denigrate Washington.

The Long Winter

When the Continental Army went into winter quarters at Valley Forge in 1777–78, it was woefully short of supplies. To remedy the shortage, effective March 24, 1778, Washington named Greene as the army's quartermaster, whose job it was to make sure the troops were supplied with food, clothing, quarters, and equipment. Greene accepted the position reluctantly. Nevertheless, he performed the job admirably after extracting a promise from Washington that he would be in command of troops when needed.

True to his word, Washington assigned Greene to command troops at the June 28, 1778, battle at Monmouth, New Jersey. He also named Greene commanding officer at West Point, a post Benedict Arnold had vacated.

REVOLUTIONARY REVELATIONS

Greene was a fair man. Once André admitted that he was a spy, the Americans had little choice but to hang him for his treachery. However, Greene met with the British General James Robertson after the sentence was pronounced to listen to arguments to save André's life. He considered them carefully, but ultimately rejected them. André was hanged.

Greene arrived at West Point shortly after John André's and Benedict Arnold's plot to turn the site over to the British was revealed. He stayed at West Point long enough to strengthen its defenses and chair the commission to try André. Then he was reassigned to a new theater.

Greene Heads South

As 1780 neared, the Americans needed a talented, aggressive army commander in the Deep South, where the British had won a series of significant victories in 1779. General Horatio Gates was not up to the task. Washington sent Greene to replace him.

Quotations to Live (and Die) By!

"WHAT I HAVE BEEN DREADING HAS COME TO PASS. HIS EXCELLENCY GENERAL WASHINGTON HAS APPOINTED ME TO COMMAND OF THE SOUTHERN ARMY . . . THIS IS SO FOREIGN FROM MY WISHES THAT I AM DISTRESSED EXCEEDINGLY . . . HOW UNFRIENDLY WAR IS TO DOMESTIC HAPPINESS!"

—NATHANAEL GREENE IN AN OCTOBER 1780 LETTER TO HIS WIFE CATHERINE

Greene arrived at Charlotte, North Carolina, on December 2, 1780. Due to his perennial shortage of men and supplies, he played cat-and-mouse with the British army for several months. He finally lured them into a battle at Guilford Court House on March 14, 1781. The Americans did not win the battle, but they damaged the British considerably. The British sustained 532 casualties, considerably more than the American total of 365.

Greene then began a systematic withdrawal across South Carolina that further weakened the British, who were getting farther and farther away from their supply sources as they followed him.

The British commander, General Cornwallis, fell into Greene's trap. The two sides met again in battle at Hobkirk's Hill, Ninety Six, Eutaw Springs—always places of Greene's choosing. Finally, after the battle of Eutaw Springs on September 8, 1781, Cornwallis realized the futility of his chase. Greene had won the war without winning a battle. Greene left South Carolina in August 1783, secure in the knowledge that he had been instrumental in securing independence for the United States.

REVOLUTIONARY REVELATIONS

Greene did not leave the South empty-handed. The North Carolina legislature gave him 5,000 guineas, and Georgia presented him with 24,000 acres of prime real estate—and a place to be buried.

Back to Georgia

Once the war ended, Greene returned to Rhode Island, which no longer held the fascination it once had for him. He had some valuable land in Georgia, so he moved the family there in late 1785. Life was idyllic for them.

Sadly, the beauty was not to last. While visiting a fellow planter in early June 1786, Greene stayed out in the sun too long. He became feverish and died a few days later. The country went into mourning for the man who had stayed so loyal to George Washington and his country throughout the war—and can truly be credited with helping to save both.

ALEXANDER HAMILTON

Caribbean Island of Nevis
January 11, 1755 or 1757–July 12, 1804
Duel Personalities

Hamilton's accomplishments overshadowed his sometimes acerbic personality. He was a financial genius whose work as the first secretary of the treasury set a precedent that was hard to follow. The list of legislative bodies in which he served was long and varied. Hamilton established the U.S. Mint and the Revenue Cutter Service, the forerunner of the U.S. Coast Guard. He might have accomplished more for his adopted country had he not been cut down at a relatively early age in a duel.

Beating the Odds

Of all the Founding Fathers, Alexander Hamilton had the largest hill to climb to reach success. Most of them were born into aristocratic families. Hamilton was a poor, illegitimate child whose father lived thousands of miles away.

Alexander Hamilton's mother, Rachel Faucett Lavien, was married to John Lavien. They lived on the Danish island of St. Croix. Rachel and John divorced in 1759. According to Danish law, she could not remarry. Rachel moved to Nevis, where she met James Hamilton. They produced Alexander and moved to St. Croix in 1765. So, by a quirk of law, Alexander was an illegitimate child. Shortly thereafter, James abandoned his family, leaving Rachel to rely on friends and family members for financial support.

After she died in 1768, islanders saw to it that Hamilton learned to read, write, and learn the mercantile business. Once they determined that he was exceptionally bright, they sent him to New York for a proper education at King's College (now Columbia University). He was fifteen at the time.

Hamilton arrived in New York when debates over independence versus loyalty to Britain were reaching a fever pitch. He got into the spirit of the debates in a pamphlet battle with a loyalist who was writing under the pseudonym "The Farmer." Hamilton rebutted "The Farmer's" arguments, using the name "Friend to America." The die was cast: Hamilton was firmly in the patriots' corner, and he did not hesitate to blast Parliament.

FEDERAL FACTS

Debates were often waged in written form in the 1700s. Writers using pen names squared off through widely read pamphlets that served as starting points for pro and con supporters to argue.

Firing for Effect

While engaging in debate, Hamilton was also preparing for war. He immersed himself in a study of artillery warfare. His self-training paid off quickly: Hamilton joined an artillery regiment in March 1776, and received an officer's commission as captain of the Provincial Company of Artillery. The title sounded more impressive than the job actually was. Before he could resolve all his logistics challenges, such as outfitting, arming, and training his troops, Hamilton was embroiled in the war.

General Washington moved his troops from Boston to New York and the battles around the city involved Hamilton's New York Artillery Regiment. He turned out to be a fine artillery officer.

For the next few years, Hamilton fought in battle after battle. He took a position as an aide to General Washington, but they had a falling out because Washington would not give Hamilton his own command.

Washington relented eventually. Hamilton had his own command during the siege of Yorktown in 1781, where he led the Americans in the final attack on the British position. After the campaign ended, the fighting subsided and the need for an active army diminished. Hamilton ended his active military career as a result, and returned to New York to study law. He was appointed to Congress and saw another side of the military: the lack of financial support for the army. Hamilton served one year in the Continental Congress, then concentrated on his law practice. In his "spare" time he established the Bank of New York.

FEDERAL FACTS

Men who raised their own militia units in the Revolutionary War era were responsible for recruiting, training, feeding, and supplying their troops, as well as leading them in battle.

A National Treasurer

Hamilton did not stay on the political sidelines for long. He saw a need for centralization and checks and balances in government. Consequently, he was named a delegate from New York to the 1786 Annapolis Convention, which required a good chunk of his time. The Annapolis Convention was convened to discuss the Articles of Confederation, the United States' first attempt at governing itself. The result of the gathering was a recommendation to forget the articles and write a new Constitution.

After the convention failed to accomplish its goal, a call went out for delegates to a Constitutional Convention. Hamilton served as a delegate. He helped draft the Constitution and wrote many of the "Federalist Papers," eighty-five essays written under pseudonyms between October

1787 and August 1788 by Hamilton, John Jay, and James Madison in support of ratification of the U.S. Constitution.

After the Constitution was ratified, Hamilton served in the Congress of the Confederation in 1788–89. But Washington called on him once again, naming him the nation's first secretary of the treasury.

Quotations to Live (and Die) By!

"A NATIONAL DEBT, IF IT IS NOT EXCESSIVE, WILL BE TO US A NATIONAL BLESSING."
—ALEXANDER HAMILTON

Hamilton believed in a strong federal government. He maintained that the U.S. Constitution—which he had helped write—allowed the federal government to fund the national debt, assume state debts, and create its own bank. He proposed that these programs would be funded by a tariff on imports and an excise tax on whiskey.

The End of Hamilton's Public Service Career

It wasn't Hamilton's controversial views about the role of the federal government that did him in. It was a foolish moral lapse that led to his resignation from his position and ended his public service career.

Hamilton was the male star of the nation's first major political sex scandal. He had a two-year affair with Maria Lewis Reynolds, the wife of one of his acquaintances, James Reynolds. Mr. Reynolds knew about the affair; he used it to blackmail Hamilton, with Maria's complicity. Hamilton made at least two payments to satisfy Reynolds's demands. Eventually, Hamilton admitted his role in the affair to two congressional investigators, James Monroe and Frederick Muhlenberg. They handled the matter discreetly, and it was relegated to old news. The federal government had weathered its first real political scandal.

After the investigation ended, Hamilton went back to his law practice and never held national office again. But he kept interfering in national political affairs. He helped engineer Thomas Jefferson's election as president in 1800 in order to spite his old nemesis, John Adams, who had no love for Hamilton.

Adams and Hamilton engaged in a constant struggle for the leadership of the Federalist Party. During Adams's presidency, Hamilton sought constantly to advise his cabinet members, which aggravated the president. Hamilton exacerbated the rift between them close to the election of 1800 when he attacked Adams's policies in a document intended for private circulation, titled *The Public Conduct and Character of John Adams, Esq., President of the United States.*

In the document, Hamilton included confidential information about Adams's cabinet activities. Aaron Burr, Hamilton's legal and political adversary and Jefferson's vice-presidential running mate, published a copy of the treatise without Hamilton's knowledge. Burr's duplicity heightened the animosity between him and Hamilton.

Quotations to Live (and Die) By!

"This bastard brat of a Scotch pedlar [*sic*]."
—John Adams about Alexander Hamilton

In the 1800 presidential election, Jefferson and Aaron Burr were tied in the number of electoral votes. In the House of Representatives, which would cast the deciding vote, Hamilton campaigned against Burr to help get Jefferson elected. Four years later, he again worked to keep Burr out of the White House.

Burr took exception to Hamilton's meddling in the presidential elections. He challenged Hamilton to a duel on the pretext of some alleged insults Hamilton had hurled at Burr. They met on the Weehawken, New Jersey, dueling diamond on July 11, 1804.

REVOLUTIONARY REVELATIONS

Alexander Hamilton's oldest son Philip had lost his life in a duel three years earlier—on the same ground.

Burr shot Hamilton, who died the next day. Burr killed more than a man; he killed a national treasure. Hamilton's service to the United States had been extraordinary. Sadly, the man who had done so much to build his adopted country was done in by an affair and a duel.

JOHN HANCOCK

Braintree, Massachusetts
January 12, 1737–October 8, 1793
Did He Really Say That?

John Hancock is best known for his exaggerated signature on the Declaration of Independence. But he earned the right to do that. Hancock was a successful merchant and the president of the Second Continental Congress from 1775 to 1777, when the document was adopted. Later, he served as the first governor of the commonwealth of Massachusetts from 1780–1785 and 1787–1793, and served as the inspiration for an insurance company.

Me, in Politics?

As a young man, John Hancock was not interested in politics. Running a business was his primary interest. After graduating from Harvard in 1754, Hancock began an apprenticeship at his uncle's retail and shipping business, which he inherited in 1764. By then he was increasingly opposed to the growing number of British acts aimed at raising tax revenues from the colonists.

In 1764, Hancock cofounded the local Society to Encourage Trade. Subsequently, he was elected to one of Boston's seven selectmen seats in 1765. When news of the impending Stamp Act reached the colonies, Hancock seemed uninterested. He had other problems to deal with: His balance sheet was a mess, he had very little cash, and his suppliers refused to let him operate on credit.

Quotations to Live (and Die) By!

"I SELDOM MEDDLE WITH POLITICKS, & INDEED HAVE
NOT TIME NOW TO SAY ANYTHING ON THAT HEAD."
—JOHN HANCOCK

By the time the Stamp Act became effective, Hancock owed one supplier alone £19,000. American trade was stagnant, and merchants vigorously protested the Stamp Act. At this point, his financial distress was great enough that Hancock joined the growing number of protesters. Samuel Adams befriended Hancock, supported his bid for selectman, introduced him to members of the patriot clubs, and invited him to a few secret meetings. Suddenly, John found himself in a position to exert influence. Other merchants looked to him for guidance.

Meddling in Politics Becomes a Passion

Hancock informed his agents in London that he would no longer import British goods until the Stamp Act was repealed, which it was, on March 18, 1766.

Hancock became an active leader in the fight against British taxation policies. Tensions came to a head on June 10, 1768, when British commissioners seized his sloop *Liberty*, alleging that he had not paid taxes on his entire cargo of wine.

A mob assembled on the wharf to support Hancock. As the drama played out, the mob became more agitated and rowdy. Patriots seized a boat owned by one of the commissioners and burned it near Hancock's mansion as their leaders urged the crowd to "take up arms and be free." Hancock helped disperse the crowd before it became more riled. The *Liberty* affair bolstered his growing popularity.

The war between Hancock and the customs commissioners was not over. On November 3, 1768, he was arrested for smuggling. John Adams defended Hancock in court. Despite irregular proceedings by the prosecution, Hancock was acquitted and became more of a public hero than ever.

The stress of the court proceedings over his arrest for smuggling and the public horror over the Boston Massacre convinced him that inflammatory politics were not the best way to fight British taxation policies—until Britain passed the Tea Act of 1773.

The Last Straw

The tea tax was Parliament's effort to save the faltering East India Company, an English joint stock firm, by selling its tea in Boston at a bargain price. Bostonians protested the act by dressing up as Indians and dumping the tea into the harbor on the night of December 16, 1773. Hancock did not play a direct role in the protest. He did attend a meeting earlier that night at which he spoke and told everyone there to do what they thought was right.

Tensions in Boston ran high. In 1775, General Thomas Gage, the new military royal governor of Massachusetts, ordered his soldiers to fortify the town's defenses and canceled a General Assembly meeting of the Provincial Congress slated to convene in nearby Salem.

Defiant congressional delegates met anyway. They established the Massachusetts Committee of Safety, charged with forming a 15,000-man army and securing supplies, arms, and artillery. Hancock, convinced war was imminent, settled his debts with his London agent, and went into the revolution still cash poor, but ready for action.

★ ★ ★ ★ ★ ★ ★ ★ ★ ★ ★ ★ ★

FEDERAL FACTS

British troops received copies of a handbill that identified the troublemakers who were responsible for inciting public sentiment against the British government. The handbill included Hancock's name.

Hancock was reelected to the Provincial Congress and selected as a delegate to the Second Continental Congress. His activities set him even more firmly in the sights of the occupying British forces. General Thomas Gage ordered the seizure of the Boston Safety Committee's munitions. The stage for war was set.

REVOLUTIONARY REVELATIONS

Hancock was so busy that he postponed his marriage to Dorothy Quincy, a young lady of prominent social stature selected for him by his Aunt Lydia. He wrote to Dorothy to explain his attentions were required elsewhere and promised to "return as soon as possible," hoping she would not be "saucy" when he did. They married eventually.

Hancock was elected president of the Second Continental Congress. He successfully walked the fine line between the radicals who desired independence and moderates who favored reconciliation. In the process, he incurred the enmity of John Adams and Samuel Adams, who tried to curtail his growing power and influence. They believed that Hancock's vanity and lavish lifestyle did not set a good example for people who were struggling to establish a new country and sacrificing material goods and personal wealth in the process.

Hancock learned by May 1776 that he had been deliberately excluded from the Massachusetts

FEDERAL FACTS

When John Hancock volunteered to be commander in chief of the Continental Army, John Adams and Samuel Adams supported George Washington. By 1776, the rift deepened between Hancock and the Adamses. The cousins tried to undermine any future Hancock planned in Massachusetts politics by securing a coalition that excluded him and attacked his allies and associates.

lower house and the Governor's Council. Seeing the mood of the times and the radicals moving into popular sentiment, he became an ardent convert to the cause of independence.

Hancock's father-in-law, Edmund Quincy, advised him after the British left Boston that "Nothing will answer the end so well as a Declaration to all the world for absolute Independency." Hancock took that advice, as his large signature on the Declaration demonstrates. While he is purported to have said, "There, I guess King George will be able to read that" about his signature, there is no definitive proof that he actually uttered those words or anything like them.

★ ★ ★ ★ ★ ★ ★ ★ ★ ★ ★ ★ ★

FEDERAL FACTS

The Declaration of Independence was signed starting on August 2, 1776; not all fifty-six signers were present that day. There was some rhyme and reason to the order in which the delegates signed the document. John Hancock signed first because he was the president of the Congress. The other fifty-five delegates signed by state, arranged from the northernmost state (New Hampshire) to the southernmost (Georgia).

★ ★ ★ ★ ★ ★ ★ ★ ★ ★ ★ ★ ★

Return to Massachusetts

After Congress approved the Declaration of Independence, Hancock returned to Boston to renew his political aspirations and earn some money. He feared that he might be attacked en route from Philadelphia to Boston. So, in a typical example of the Hancock extravagances that riled John and Samuel Adams, he requested an armed escort from George Washington, who provided him with fifteen horsemen.

Shortly after his return, Hancock was elected as governor of Massachusetts by a landslide. Hancock spent his gubernatorial career largely as a figurehead, with enough sense to let the powers of the legislature have their way.

Hancock served additional terms as governor of Massachusetts and was elected to the Massachusetts convention to ratify the U.S.

Constitution. He had hopes of serving as the first president of the United States, but realized the national political current would not support him.

His career ended prematurely. Hancock was fifty-six years old when he died, ending his career as a master politician. His place in history will always rest on his large signature on the Declaration of Independence.

BENJAMIN HARRISON

Berkeley, Virginia
April 5, 1726–April 24, 1791
Virginia's Odd Man Out

Benjamin Harrison was the stereotypical unsung hero of the Revolutionary War era. His accomplishments were overshadowed by those of some of his contemporary Virginia politicians of note, such as Thomas Jefferson, James Madison, and James Monroe. Nevertheless, his contributions were noteworthy. He served in the Virginia House of Burgesses (the colony's legislature) and the Continental Congress; was governor of Virginia; signed the Declaration of Independence; distinguished himself as a member of the Board of War; and advised the Virginia delegation on how to strengthen the U.S. Constitution by adding necessary amendments. He did it all quietly, but persuasively, despite the lack of recognition he has received from historians over the years.

Sixth Man

Benjamin Harrison was like the sixth man on a basketball team. The starting five included George Wythe, Thomas Jefferson, Richard Henry Lee, Francis Lightfoot Lee, and Carter Braxton. Harrison would have started on a lot of other teams, but historians focused more on his contemporaries because of their credentials.

One of the major differences between Harrison and his Virginia peers in the lead-up to the Revolutionary War was his age. With the exception of Wythe, Harrison was older than most of the Virginia delegates at the First Continental Congress. Wythe and Harrison were both born in 1726.

A second difference was education. Although Harrison had matriculated at William & Mary College, he did not graduate, as did most young men from affluent families in Virginia at the time. That explains in part why he was not elected to the Virginia House of Burgesses until he was nearly thirty years old, which gave him a late start in politics.

REVOLUTIONARY REVELATIONS

While Benjamin Harrison was away at college, his father and two sisters were struck and killed by lightning. The young man cut his studies short and returned home to manage the family's estate.

Harrison spent most of his youth managing the family's large estate following his father's death. That did not give him time to fulfill the political obligations that were almost mandatory for young men from aristocratic families at the time. But he did not like what he was seeing in the 1760s, as the British government passed acts aimed at siphoning off Americans' money. Thus, he was eager to curb what he felt were Britain's infringements on Americans' freedom.

Harrison took the initial step toward that goal in 1756 when he was elected to the Virginia House of Burgesses for the first time. He served a two-year term as a representative from Surry County, then took an eight-year hiatus. Harrison was elected again in 1766 to represent Charles City County. He became a leader in the house. That was a double-edged sword for him.

The pro-independence and the loyalist factions in Virginia both wanted him on their side.

Virginia's Royal Lieutenant Governor Francis Fauquier tried to seduce Harrison into accepting an appointment to his Executive Council in

1765 after the House of Burgesses passed its anti–Stamp Act resolutions in defiance of the act. Harrison turned down the offer, telling Fauquier he preferred to act according to republican principles.

Harrison made it plain to his fellow delegates that he wanted to end Britain's right to rule over the Americans. His toast at a dinner on September 2, 1774, made that clear: "A constitutional death to the Lords Bute, Mansfield and North." Why he included Bute was a mystery. He had been King George III's confidant and prime minister, but he had resigned in 1763. Mansfield and North were legitimate political targets, however. Mansfield was the lord chief justice of the King's Bench, and North was the chancellor of the exchequer. They were influential officials who were instrumental in developing and implementing Parliament's tax legislation.

On the Whole . . .

Harrison was occasionally named to chair the prestigious Committee of the Whole at the Second Continental Congress, a revolving appointment. One of those times was in 1776. As such, he was privy to deliberations, communications, and decisions regarding a variety of matters, ranging from General Washington's dispatches to the regulation of trade and the overall state of the colonies. His evenhanded approach and calm demeanor made him an effective leader, especially as a member and chairman of the Board of War created in 1776 to oversee the American army and the conduct of the war.

Toward the end of the Revolutionary War, Harrison was reelected to the Virginia House of Burgesses and named Speaker.

Harrison left the House of Burgesses in 1782 after being elected as governor of Virginia. He was reelected twice, which was the maximum number of times he could serve as governor. But he was not through serving Virginia.

REVOLUTIONARY REVELATIONS

Benjamin Harrison served on the Second Continental Congress's Committee of Secret Correspondence in 1776 with Benjamin Franklin, John Dickinson, John Jay, Robert Morris, and Thomas Johnson of Maryland.

Based on his history and reputation, Benjamin Harrison was elected to Virginia's Constitution ratification committee. He was not a proponent of the document, because it did not contain a bill of rights.

Virginia took an unusual two-step approach to ratifying the U.S. Constitution. Step one was the declaration of ratification. Step two was a recommendation that a bill of rights be added.

Perhaps because of his opposition to the Constitution as written, and certainly in deference to his ill health at the time, Harrison did not take an active part in the debate. However, he served on a committee charged with drafting a sample bill of rights.

Harrison had two more opportunities to serve his fellow Virginians after the ratification. The first was another term as governor, which he turned down. The second was in the state legislature. He was elected to that body in April 1791. He died the day after the election.

In the long run, Harrison was every bit as effective as his better known contemporaries. He proved, however, that the people who helped gain independence did not have to be ostentatious. All they had to be was dedicated and industrious—as he was.

FEDERAL FACTS

Benjamin Harrison's son, William Henry Harrison, won election as the ninth president of the United States. He died in office after serving less than a month. He earned the distinctions of being the first U.S. president to die in office and the shortest serving president.

⊱ PATRICK HENRY ⊰

Hanover County, Virginia
May 29, 1736 – June 6, 1799
Master of Sound Bites

When Patrick Henry spoke, people listened. And he had plenty of opportunities to speak. He was a lawyer, legislator, five-term governor of Virginia, and a vociferous proponent of the right to bear arms. Most importantly, he was a champion for liberty and America's greatest cheerleader for independence. His name is attached to ships, monuments, and other public structures. Henry may not be the most famous Founding Father, but his quotes are among the most recognized.

A Self-Taught Lawyer

Patrick Henry's father, John, provided him with homeschooling that included a background in Latin. When it came to learning law, Patrick taught himself. He also acquired well-developed persuasive skills as a youth, which came in handy when he took his bar examination and throughout his political life.

Even though he had no formal training in the law, Henry easily passed his bar exam in 1760. He set up a practice in Williamsburg, Virginia, which flourished quickly.

Henry came to prominence in 1763 when he argued the Parson's Cause in Hanover County, which was one of the first indications of a schism between Britain and the colonies. The case involved the relationship

110

between tobacco and Anglican clergymen's pay. A 1748 Virginia law allowed the clergymen to be paid in tobacco—16,000 pounds each per year. Normally, the market price for tobacco was two cents a pound. That is what the clergymen grew accustomed to, even though they thought they were underpaid. But due to droughts in 1759 and 1760, the market price of tobacco soared when the scarcity of the product created a seller's market. That created a conflict with the unpopular Two Penny Act the Virginia House of Burgesses had passed in 1758, which mandated that debts in tobacco were to be paid in currency at two pennies per pound. The ramifications of the law upset the clergymen in the early 1760s; they thought they should be paid according to the higher market price. The clergymen appealed to British authorities, and King George vetoed the bill. The Virginia legislators interpreted the veto as an infringement on their right to self-rule.

One clergyman, James Maury, sued the county on his counterparts' behalf for back pay to compensate for the uptick in the market price of tobacco in 1759 and 1760. Patrick Henry, still a novice attorney at the time, argued the county's case. He focused on British interference in local politics as a central issue in the case, claiming that local law took precedence, and urged the jury to award Maury only one penny in damages. He was vociferous against British interference in his oratories during the trial.

 Quotations to Live (and Die) By!

"A KING, BY DISALLOWING ACTS OF THIS SALUTARY NATURE, FROM BEING THE FATHER OF HIS PEOPLE, DEGENERATED INTO A TYRANT AND FORFEITS ALL RIGHT TO HIS SUBJECTS' OBEDIENCE."
—PATRICK HENRY

In the end, the jury agreed with him. Henry won the case for the county and the clergy gave up their protest. Young Henry earned a reputation as an outspoken critic of British interference in domestic issues and established a pattern of arguing for the colonies' right to independence. From that point on, Henry was in demand as a lawyer. The next step in his career was entering the political stage.

Patrick the Politician

In 1765, Henry was elected to the House of Burgesses, where he became an ardent supporter of the right to bear arms. The young firebrand was not popular at first, especially when he introduced five resolutions against the Stamp Act on May 30, 1765. The burgesses were for the most part still loyal to the king, and many of them considered Henry a traitor. He won them over, though, and the burgesses adopted four of his resolutions. Henry's persuasive skills had nudged Virginia down the path to rebellion and independence. Moreover, he established his position as Virginia's leader in its battle for independence.

Quotations to Live (and Die) By!

"THE GREAT OBJECT IS, THAT EVERY MAN BE ARMED."
—PATRICK HENRY

For the next ten years, Henry urged his fellow Virginians to throw off their allegiance to the king and push for their independence. He advised them to arm themselves, especially after word reached Virginia about the skirmishes between British troops and Massachusetts patriots.

Henry expanded his sphere of influence outside Virginia in the 1770s. He was one of Virginia's seven delegates to the First Continental Congress. Henry was assigned to several committees, but it was his speaking skills that earned him notice when he introduced the idea of a unified America.

Quotations to Live (and Die) By!

"THE DISTINCTIONS BETWEEN VIRGINIANS, PENNSYLVA-
NIANS, NEW YORKERS, AND NEW ENGLANDERS, ARE NO
MORE. I AM NOT A VIRGINIAN, BUT AN AMERICAN."

—PATRICK HENRY AT THE FIRST CONTINENTAL CONGRESS IN 1774

Henry hit the high mark of his oratorical skills in March 1775 in his famous "Give me liberty or give me death" speech in Richmond, Virginia. The words he used were typical of his pleas to Virginians to arm themselves for self-defense. His views were remarkable, since Henry was a Quaker, and Quakers were (and are) pacifists.

 Quotations to Live (and Die) By!

"IS LIFE SO DEAR, OR PEACE SO SWEET, AS TO BE PUR-
CHASED AT THE PRICE OF CHAINS OR SLAVERY? FORBID
IT, ALMIGHTY GOD! I KNOW NOT WHAT COURSE OTHERS
MAY TAKE; BUT AS FOR ME, GIVE ME LIBERTY OR GIVE
ME DEATH!"

—PATRICK HENRY AT ST. JOHN'S CHURCH, RICHMOND, VIRGINIA,
MARCH 23, 1775

Virginia's royal governor John Dunmore, fearing an armed rebellion, ordered the removal of some gunpowder from a Williamsburg magazine. Henry the orator morphed into Henry the militia leader. Shortly after the British marched on Concord, Massachusetts, Henry forced Dunmore to return the gunpowder. Any chance of a reconciliation between the two leaders ended. Dunmore returned to England in July 1776. He retained his title, but his authority left the colonies with him.

A Statesman, Not a Soldier

Henry had a brief military career during the Revolutionary War, but he never served in the field. Since he did not have any significant military experience, that was probably a good thing. His peers were sure he would be more valuable as a statesman.

Henry served as Virginia's governor from 1776 to 1779, and again from 1784 to 1786. In the interim, he was a member of the Virginia House of Delegates. One of his preoccupations in the 1780s was fighting ratification of the proposed U.S. Constitution. Henry favored strong state governments and a weak federal government, whereas the U.S. Constitution being offered advocated just the opposite. It passed despite his opposition.

FEDERAL FACTS

Virginia became the tenth state to ratify the U.S. Constitution via an 89–79 vote on June 25, 1788.

Patrick Henry's spirit was sorely missed in Virginia after his death in 1799. Even though he had performed most of his public service in his home state, his contributions were felt nationally—and the words for which he is best known, "Give me liberty or give me death," still resonate today.

JOSEPH HEWES

Kingston, New Jersey
January 23, 1730 – November 10, 1779
Man of Mystery

Joseph Hewes worked tirelessly in the background for his country while keeping the details of his life a closely guarded secret. He became an expert on maritime affairs while building a shipping business and worked tirelessly on committees to share his knowledge in the best interests of the country, especially its fledgling navy. Hewes went so far as to renounce his Quaker religion and sacrifice a large part of his business to promote independence. His early, adamant opposition to independence set him apart from many of the Founding Fathers. But he eventually came around to their way of thinking.

Hewes the Delegate

By the time he was thirty years old, the young Princeton graduate was a wealthy man living in New Jersey, where he had acquired a reputation as an honorable and ethical businessman. Despite his early success in New Jersey, Hewes moved to North Carolina in 1760 and launched successful shipping and merchant businesses in Wilmington. Within three years he was elected to the North Carolina legislature and was on his way to a successful political career.

In 1775, the royal governor of North Carolina dissolved the colony's provincial legislature. Hewes, a Quaker and an outspoken critic of the British government but a proponent of reconciliation rather than independence, had been a member of the legislature for nine years by that time. North Carolinians disenchanted with British legislation issued a notice on February 11, 1775, requesting the election of representatives for a shadow provincial congress to be held on April 3rd. On March 1, 1775, Governor Josiah Martin informed his council that such proceedings were "highly derogatory to the dignitary of the Legislature, which had been appointed to meet on the same day, and in every light illegal, and inconsistent with good order and government."

The North Carolina patriots defied Martin and created a separate legislature. Hewes went on to represent North Carolina at the ongoing Second Continental Congress in Philadelphia in 1775, and again in 1776, along with William Hooper and John Penn.

The North Carolina Provincial Congress, the colony's shadow legislature, provided clear instructions to its delegates. It told Hewes, Hooper, and Penn "to concur with the delegates of other colonies in declaring Independence and to form foreign alliances."

A Tireless, Quiet Worker

Joseph Hewes was an anomaly at the Second Continental Congress. Instructions to the contrary, he was firmly anti-independence at the beginning, even though he disagreed with British tax policies. He tried to convince pro-independence delegates that the country did not have to separate from Britain to get the relief they wanted from Parliament.

Hewes was not always successful in getting his points across, though, because he did not possess well-refined persuasive skills. Therefore, when he tried to convince his peers that independence was not the way to go, they often laughed at or scolded him. So he stopped talking and started working on committees instead. Strangely enough, he generally worked with committees that favored independence. Finally, he had an epiphany and accepted independence as a solution.

In the end, he had to make personal sacrifices to support his principles. As a Quaker, he was expected to abide by pacifist beliefs.

Early in 1775, the Society of Friends (the Quakers) held a convention to denounce the congress meeting in Philadelphia. Not only did they oppose war, they also opposed the committees formed by delegates at the Second Continental Congress.

As a result, Hewes broke his affiliation with the Quakers in favor of independence, committee work—and war. In so doing, he acted on both his religious and political convictions.

Even though he was not always willing to put his mouth to work in Congress, Hewes was willing to put his money where his mouth was. That, more than anything, set him apart from other members of the group.

 Quotations to Live (and Die) By!

"IT IS DONE! AND I WILL ABIDE BY IT."

—JOSEPH HEWES'S EPIPHANY ON JULY 1, 1776, AS JOHN ADAMS ARGUED FOR INDEPENDENCE

What's Mine Is Yours

In 1774 the First Continental Congress had recommended a system of nonimportation to hit the British in their pocketbooks. The suggestion had not gained much traction between then and 1776. Hewes changed that. He and some of his counterparts worked to develop a nonimportation association.

Belonging to the nonimportation association was costly for Hewes. A large chunk of his business involved imports from British merchants, with whom he had been dealing for over twenty years. When Hewes gave them up voluntarily, it cost him a considerable amount of money.

Hewes also put his ships at the new country's disposal. In one of those little coincidences of history that rarely—if ever—get into history books, Hewes pushed hard to get a navy commander's assignment for his friend John Paul Jones. And Jones went on to become the country's first naval hero. Hewes's knowledge of maritime affairs was invaluable to the Americans. In 1776, he offered his ships to the Continental armed forces.

Hewes served on a committee to rig the first navy ship and as the secretary of the Naval Affairs Committee until 1779. As a result of his work, he can be considered the "Father of the Navy," although he has stiff competition for the claim from people like Jeremiah O'Brien and John Paul Jones.

By the time Hewes signed the Declaration of Independence, he had given the country a lot more than his time. He had provided ships, sacrificed part of his business, brought John Paul Jones's name to the attention of military leaders, and denounced his Quaker heritage. Sadly, he would not live to see his dedication pay off.

No Airs, No Heirs

Hewes was tired and ill when he signed the Declaration of Independence. He went home afterward to settle some of his business and private affairs and serve with the North Carolina legislature. Hewes was reelected to Congress again in 1779, and returned to Philadelphia.

REVOLUTIONARY REVELATIONS

Few people knew much about Hewes's private affairs. The soft-spoken man was a lifelong bachelor, only because his fiancée, Isabella Johnston, died a few days before their wedding. Thus, he had no heirs to carry on his family name—or his history.

On October 29, 1779, Hewes fell ill and never recovered. He died on November 10. The entire Congress attended his funeral the next day, along with the general assembly of Pennsylvania, its president and supreme executive council, the minister plenipotentiary of France, and a large number of citizens.

The ceremony was a fitting send-off for a man whom few people actually knew well, and whom history books seldom mention. All they knew was that he had given up a lot to help create the United States, which was a price he was willing to pay.

FEDERAL FACTS

Congress resolved to wear crepe armbands for one month in honor of Joseph Hewes after his death.

If there was anyone at the Second Continental Congress who was familiar with the tempestuous history between Britain and the American colonies, it was Stephen Hopkins. Hopkins was not only an educator and a student of the history between them, he had lived it. The self-educated Hopkins was sixty-nine years old on the day he signed the Declaration of Independence, and well versed in how badly the relationships between Britain and America had been deteriorating for years. Hopkins was not averse to keeping the political pot boiling by stirring up his fellow patriots against the Crown and always being ready to defend the colonies against its domineering laws and policies. He was one of the first patriots to advocate a "United States" long before the call for independence became fashionable.

Hopkins the Writer

Stephen Hopkins, a farmer in his youth, held several political offices in his hometown of Scituate, such as the town clerk, justice of the peace, and president of the town council. He served in the Rhode Island General Assembly from 1732–52, acting as Speaker from 1738–44 and again in 1749. Significantly, Hopkins was an early advocate of uniting the colonies. He supported Ben Franklin's plan to consolidate the northern colonies in 1755, his first year as governor of Rhode Island. After a meeting in Albany, New York, attended by delegates from seven of the thirteen colonies, he wrote *A True Representation of the Plan Formed at Albany for Uniting All the British Northern Colonies.*

The Albany Congress had been convened to discuss unifying the colonies. While it was adjourned before any agreement was reached, it laid the groundwork for the Continental Congress in 1776.

Hopkins's second major treatise, *The Rights of the Colonies Examined*, was published in 1765. In it he analyzed Parliament's authority and justified colonial opposition to it. He did not suggest in his document that the colonies break away from Britain. He expressed a wish in his conclusion that the king and his consorts gain a little wisdom in the way they ruled the colonies and "perpetuate the sovereignty of the British constitution, and the final dependency and happiness of all the colonies." If that required drastic action on the colonists' part, so be it.

Hopkins the Instigator

Hopkins played a central role in what might be considered the first actual military battle of the Revolutionary War, the *Gaspee* incident. History books don't often assign it the importance it deserves—if they mention it at all. In 1772, the British customs schooner *Gaspee*, commanded by Lieutenant William Dudingston, entered Rhode Island waters to enforce unpopular trade regulations. The ship ran aground. On June 10, 1772, about 100 local patriots boarded, burned, and sank the *Gaspee*, shot and wounded Dudingston, and captured the crew. The British did not take kindly to the incident. They threatened to identify the miscreants, ship them to England, and try them for treason.

Hopkins, the chief justice of the Rhode Island Superior Court at the time, made a show of cooperating with the British. He promised to provide the British commission investigating the incident with a full written account of his own findings. There is no evidence that he ever did—or ever intended to comply with the commission's demands.

> **REVOLUTIONARY REVELATIONS**
>
> Hopkins suggested early in 1772 that no British ship should be operating in or near Rhode Island without permission, as he told the colony's deputy governor.

In fact, he leveled a threat of his own. Hopkins implied that he might arrest Dudingston. He issued a warrant for Dudingston's arrest in October 1773, but he did not follow up on it.

A little over a year after the incident took place, Hopkins made it clear that he had no serious intention of prosecuting anyone for burning a British ship. The incident became a national issue when Thomas Jefferson urged committees of correspondence in other colonies to coordinate a united response to the British should they attempt to punish the miscreants who attacked the *Gaspee*. They never did, although the British offered a reward of £1,000 to anyone who would turn them in, which was magnanimous, since the ship cost only £545 to build and outfit. That demonstrated how seriously the British took the incident, although Hopkins did not. He moved on.

Hopkins's Crowning Achievement

Hopkins started serving with the First Continental Congress in 1774. When the discussion about the Declaration of Independence began in 1776, he was eager to participate.

Thus, when the delegates lined up to sign the Declaration of Independence, Stephen Hopkins had waited longer than most of the others for the privilege.

Quotations to Live (and Die) By!

"MY HANDS TREMBLE, BUT MY HEART DOES NOT."

—STEPHEN HOPKINS, ACKNOWLEDGING HIS AGE AND CEREBRAL PALSY WHEN HE SIGNED THE DECLARATION OF INDEPENDENCE

Hopkins lived for another nine years after signing the declaration. He left the Continental Congress in 1778, returned to Rhode Island, and served in its legislature from 1777–79. The man from the smallest colony left a huge impression on the people and the country he left behind.

John Jay had one of the sharpest pens in the patriots' arsenal. He fired his first cursive shot with an *Address to the People of Great Britain* in 1774. Jay continued his attacks on paper as a delegate to the First and Second Continental Congresses; chief justice of New York; minister to Spain; secretary of foreign affairs; chief justice of the U.S. Supreme Court; and governor of New York. His pen never ran out of ink, and his words almost always hit their target—as did his actions. But he didn't exactly endear himself to Americans when he negotiated the Treaty of Amity, Commerce, and Navigation with the British in 1794, which led to the formation of political parties in the United States and affirmed the Senate's sole right to ratify treaties.

A Precocious Child

At a time when some young people were just starting their college educations, John Jay graduated from King's College in 1764 with the highest honors. He was only nineteen years old at the time. Four years later he passed the New York bar exam, which marked his entry into politics.

The Committee of Correspondence was a good place for Jay to start his political career. He made news in 1774, the year he became a member, when he politely warned the British that rebellion was a possibility in his *Address to the People of Great Britain*. He said, in part, "be not surprised . . . that we . . .

whose forefathers participated in all the rights, the liberties, and the Constitution you so justly boast of . . . should refuse to surrender them to men who found their claims on no principles of reason, and who prosecute them with a design, that by having our lives and property in their power, they may with the greater facility enslave you."

The publicity generated by his address helped get him elected to the First Continental Congress despite his youth (he was only twenty-nine when he became a delegate).

In 1775, he wrote similar addresses to the people of Canada, Jamaica, and Ireland. But in one way he became the victim of his own success. He was selected as a delegate to New York's Fourth Provincial Congress, which took him away from Philadelphia and deprived him of a chance to sign the Declaration of Independence.

Justice Is Done

New York state had big things in store for Jay. He was named as the chief justice of the state's Supreme Court in September 1777. But he was too much in demand nationally to stay there long, especially after the state made a special exception for him and sent him to the Continental Congress.

When Jay was appointed as chief justice of New York state, its constitution prohibited justices from holding any post other than in the U.S. Congress, and then only if there was a "special occasion." One arose: Vermont seceded from New York and New Hampshire in November 1778. New York sent Jay to Congress to settle territorial claims arising from the secession.

Within three days of his arrival at Congress, he was named its president.

Jay stayed in Congress for a year and then assumed the post of American ambassador to Spain. That was a steppingstone to his next major assignment in 1781: working with Benjamin Franklin, John Adams, Thomas Jefferson, and Henry Laurens to negotiate a treaty with Britain.

The original plan was to seek the guidance of the French government in the negotiations. Jay did not understand why the Americans had to rely on any foreign power for advice. He wrote a letter to Congress encouraging it to bypass French involvement and deal directly with Britain. Congress agreed. The team negotiated terms that were favorable to the United States, such as British recognition of America's independence and the formation of boundaries that would allow U.S. expansion in the west. That was a coup for the United States—and Jay.

FEDERAL FACTS

When the Treaty of Paris was signed on September 3, 1783, the most surprised people in the room were the representatives of the French and Spanish governments. They did not realize how effectively Jay and his friends had dealt with the British without their help.

No Rest for the Weary

Jay returned to the United States on July 24, 1784, to accolades and new assignments. He was elected to Congress, which named him secretary of foreign affairs. He held the position until 1790. At the same time, he used his pen to argue for ratification of the U.S. Constitution.

REVOLUTIONARY REVELATIONS

Using the pen name "Publius," Jay wrote five of the eighty-five essays known as the Federalist Papers: numbers 2, 3, 4, 5, and 64. Alexander Hamilton and James Madison wrote the others. The Federalist Papers, a series of documents that pushed for the ratification of the U.S. Constitution, appeared in two New York newspapers between October 1787 and August 1788.

President George Washington asked Jay to pick any position in his administration. Jay opted for chief justice of the U.S. Supreme Court. He remained in that position from November 1789 to June 1795, during which time Washington also asked Jay to negotiate a treaty with Britain to wrap up the loose ends left over from the Treaty of Paris. What resulted was the Treaty of Amity, Commerce, and Navigation, also known as the Jay Treaty. Americans were so displeased with the terms of the Treaty of Amity, Commerce, and Navigation they burned Jay in effigy.

According to the terms, British control of northwestern posts would be eliminated within two years, the Americans could file claims for damages from British ship seizures, and the United States was granted limited trade rights in the West Indies. Those outcomes displeased ordinary Americans, who believed it was a one-sided treaty that favored the British.

Some citizens threw stones at Alexander Hamilton in New York City to express their displeasure after he spoke in defense of the treaty; others roundly protested against President Washington for signing it. It was not Jay's finest moment.

Final Acts

After his stint on the United States Supreme Court, John Jay returned to New York, where he served two

FEDERAL FACTS

The Treaty of Amity, Commerce, and Navigation that Jay negotiated had two major impacts on American politics. It led to the formation of political parties and established the precedent by which only the Senate could approve treaties. After Congress ratified the treaty, Americans formed angry mobs and accused senators of signing a "death warrant to America's liberties." The bloc that approved the treaty was known from that point as Federalists. The senators who voted against the treaty became the Jeffersonian Republicans. When the House of Representatives asked to review the treaty, President Washington refused its request. That preserved the Senate's exclusive role in approving treaties.

terms as governor. In 1801, he decided he was more suited to farming than to public office. He retired to the land that he loved, and which he believed no one should be able to take away.

 Quotations to Live (and Die) By!

"NO POWER ON EARTH HAS A RIGHT TO TAKE OUR PROPERTY FROM US WITHOUT OUR CONSENT."
—JOHN JAY

He spent the next twenty-eight years on that farm. After writing, regulating, and ruling in support of his country for twenty-seven years, he had earned the rest. Jay had compiled a record of achievement that few of his peers could equal.

THOMAS JEFFERSON

Shadwell, Virginia
April 13, 1743–July 4, 1826
Ever the Writer

The record of public service and accomplishments Thomas Jefferson achieved in his lifetime is well documented. He entered public life in 1768 when he was elected to the Virginia House of Burgesses. Later, he attended the Continental Congress; wrote the Declaration of Independence; served as governor of Virginia; served as secretary of state, vice president and president of the United States; and coordinated the Louisiana Purchase. He made a lot of enemies along the way, which is a sure sign that he must have been doing something right at least most of the time.

A Prolific Author

There was nothing in Thomas Jefferson's early life to suggest that he was destined for greatness. He attended the College of William & Mary, studied law with George Wythe from 1762–67, inherited his father's estate, Monticello, when he was twenty-one years old, was admitted to the Virginia bar in 1767, and got elected to the colony's House of Burgesses a year later.

That was the normal path for Jefferson's peers in the mid-eighteenth century. One thing distinguished Jefferson from other young men: his cleverness with words. That became his hallmark, showcased in his first significant document *A Summary View of the Rights of British America*, in which he reminded the king of Britain that Americans had rights, too. He wrote the essay in 1774, the same year he retired from his law practice in order to pursue a political career.

Many of the ideas in that document appeared in the Declaration of Independence, which he wrote with limited help in 1776. After that, he returned to Virginia, where he devoted himself to the state's affairs.

Jefferson continued writing political documents over the next few years, revising Virginia's laws (1776) and drafting the Virginia Statute for Religious Freedom (1777) and the Bill for the More General Diffusion of Knowledge (1778) to promote education in Virginia. He also served as Virginia's governor between 1779–81.

> **REVOLUTIONARY REVELATIONS**
>
> British troops paid Jefferson a visit at his Monticello home in 1781 to capture him. A young militiaman named Jack Jouett rode around British lines to warn Jefferson that they were in the neighborhood. Jefferson escaped with ten minutes to spare.

After the war ended his political career exploded.

Evil Personified?

Following the Revolutionary War, Jefferson served in a variety of positions, including United States minister to France and secretary of state. He was the United States' first secretary of state, serving from 1790–93.

Jefferson was there to help his longtime friend George Washington through his two terms as president. They differed in some political respects: Jefferson was opposed to the formation of a national bank and the Jay Treaty, backed by Alexander Hamilton and authored by John Jay.

The political differences among the leaders prompted Jefferson to form his own party, the Democratic-Republicans. It was under that banner that Jefferson became the third president of the United States, even though, as the *Connecticut Courant* suggested, some people considered him the devil incarnate.

Quotations to Live (and Die) By!

"MURDER, ROBBERY, RAPE, ADULTERY AND INCEST WILL BE OPENLY TAUGHT AND PRACTICED, THE AIR WILL BE RENT WITH THE CRIES OF DISTRESS, THE SOIL SOAKED WITH BLOOD, AND THE NATION BLACK WITH CRIMES. WHERE IS THE HEART THAT CAN CONTEMPLATE SUCH A SCENE WITHOUT SHIVERING WITH HORROR?"

—EDITORIAL IN THE *CONNECTICUT COURANT*, COMMENTING ON WHAT WOULD HAPPEN IF THOMAS JEFFERSON WON THE PRESIDENTIAL ELECTION IN 1800

When John Adams turned over the presidency to Thomas Jefferson in 1801, it marked the first peaceful transfer of authority from one party to another in the history of the United States.

Jefferson assumed the presidency at a crucial time for the United States. France and Britain were at war again, and one of Jefferson's primary goals was to keep the United States out of the conflict. He succeeded in that, but he ended up presiding over the First Tripolitan War with the Barbary States, which were interfering with American merchant ships in the Mediterranean Sea. During the Revolutionary War, the French navy protected American merchant ships from harassment by the Barbary pirates under the terms of the 1778–1783 Treaty of Alliance between the two countries. The pirates earned their money by capturing foreign ships and holding their crews for ransom. After the war ended, the French no longer provided that protection. The Americans were on their own, and they expected help from their government. When Jefferson was inaugurated as president in 1801, the pasha of Tripoli demanded $225,000 from his administration— without even capturing a ship. Jefferson refused the pasha's demand and declared war on the Barbary States, albeit reluctantly.

FEDERAL FACTS

Two of Jefferson's crowning achievements as president were the Louisiana Purchase in 1803, which doubled the size of the United States, and his authorization of the Lewis and Clark Expedition. Meriwether Lewis and William Clark explored the land included in the Louisiana Purchase and other western territory.

For the Public Good

By 1809, when James Madison, Jefferson's friend and successor, assumed the presidency, Jefferson had completed forty years of public service. Finally, he had the opportunity to devote his time to pursuits that had fascinated him since his younger days, such as farming and science.

REVOLUTIONARY REVELATIONS

Thomas Jefferson sold his collection of nearly 7,000 books to the Library of Congress in 1815. The library needed them to replace its collection that the British army burned when it passed through Washington, D.C., during the War of 1812.

For the first time, he could devote more time to his presidency of the American Philosophical Society, which was founded in 1743 as the country's first learned society, as well as see to the distribution of his books and the foundation of a university for the people of Virginia. His establishment of the University of Virginia was a major milestone for the state. He began planning the project in 1819; it opened in 1825, the year before he died.

Jefferson, ever the writer, penned his own epitaph. On his gravestone he listed what he thought were his three most significant accomplishments: writing the Declaration of Independence, drafting the Virginia Statute for Religious Freedom, and founding the University of Virginia. They were important achievements, but his accomplishments over the course of his lifetime exceeded what can be etched on a single gravestone.

JOHN PAUL JONES

Kirkbean, Scotland
July 6, 1747–July 18, 1792
A Long Voyage Home

Jones was one of the most daring—and ill-tempered—commanders in the Continental Navy. He came to America under suspicious circumstances, which are not always included in his biographies. That did not affect his navy career or his reputation for bravery, though. Jones would not give up in a naval engagement, which inspired his sailors to be tough and determined. He is best known for his victory over the British warship *Serapis* off the coast of England. Jones took the fight to the British navy—and dared them to stop him.

REVOLUTIONARY REVELATIONS

Jones was born John Paul. He added the Jones sometime in the mid-1770s, possibly due to an incident in Tobago in 1773 in which he killed a member of his crew aboard the *Betsy*. The sailor started a mutiny. Jones let his temper get the best of him. He confronted the mutineer with a sword to force him into obedience. According to Jones, the man attacked him with a piece of wood, so he killed him in self-defense. A few days later, Jones fled Tobago, traveled to America, changed his name, and "reinvented" himself. That was his story, and he stuck to it.

An Early Start

John Paul Jones began his sailing career at the age of twelve, when he sailed to America aboard a merchant vessel named *Friendship*. Its destination was Rappahannock, Virginia, where Jones's older brother, William, lived. John Paul lived with William for a while when he was not at sea learning his trade.

Jones got his first chance to command a ship by luck. He was traveling aboard a ship, ironically named *John*, as a passenger. Both the captain and the first mate died at sea of yellow fever. Jones assumed command of the *John* and brought it safely into port. The company rewarded him by appointing him as captain of the ship. At age twenty, he had his first command.

Jones stayed at sea for a few more years with different employers. In 1773, he learned that his brother had died and left him his estate. He returned to Virginia to live.

Two years later he offered his services to the Continental Navy, writing a letter on April 25, 1775, to Joseph Hewes, Robert Morris, and Thomas Jefferson asking for a commission in the navy. Four months later, he was asked to outfit the navy's first ship, *Alfred*.

On December 7, 1775, Congress appointed him as the first first lieutenant in the Continental Navy. He was assigned to *Alfred*, commanded by Stephen Hopkins's brother, Esek. The navy offered him his own ship to command, either *Providence* or *Fly*. Jones turned down the offer and sailed aboard the *Alfred* because he believed he could learn more about seamanship and fleet maneuvers by serving as a first lieutenant on a warship under the tutelage of an experienced commander than he could by commanding his own ship.

Victory at Sea

Jones's first voyage went well. The *Alfred* sailed with an American fleet to New Providence, Nassau, where the crew captured military supplies and gunpowder. En route back to the United States, they captured two British ships and engaged an enemy warship, *Cabot*, which escaped.

Quotations to Live (and Die) By!

"I WISH TO HAVE NO CONNECTION WITH ANY SHIP THAT DOES NOT SAIL FAST FOR I INTEND TO GO IN HARM'S WAY."
—JOHN PAUL JONES

After a few routine assignments in the first half of 1776, he received a commission as captain. He quickly demonstrated why Congress and the navy had faith in him.

On September 1, 1776, while commanding *Providence*, Jones skirmished with two British warships. None of the ships were damaged. Between September 3 and September 8, he captured sixteen enemy merchant vessels off the northeast coast of America. He burned eight of them and sent the rest to port as prizes. He also destroyed a Nova Scotia fishery and wreaked havoc with shipping in the area. His string of successes, however small, deprived the British of ships, sailors, and supplies.

Quotations to Live (and Die) By!

"AN HONORABLE PEACE IS AND ALWAYS WAS MY FIRST WISH! I CAN TAKE NO DELIGHT IN THE EFFUSION OF HUMAN BLOOD; BUT, IF THIS WAR SHOULD CONTINUE, I WISH TO HAVE THE MOST ACTIVE PART IN IT."
—JOHN PAUL JONES

Jones was making a name for himself, at home, and among his British enemies.

In January 1777, Commodore Hopkins replaced Jones as commander of *Providence*. Not too long after, Jones assumed command of *Ranger*, and resumed making life miserable for British shipping into 1778.

REVOLUTIONARY REVELATIONS

Jones received a unique honor on February 14, 1778. Admiral La Motte Piquet, commanding a French squadron, gave Jones, captain of *Independence*, a thirteen-gun salute and received a nine-gun salute in return. It was the first time a foreign power ever rendered a salute to the American flag.

Older and Bolder

Sailing in foreign waters brought out the best in Jones. On April 22, 1778, he sailed into Whitehaven, on the coast of England, where he spiked guns and burned ships. The next day he visited St. Mary's Isle, intending to capture the Earl of Selkirk. The earl was not at home, so Jones contented himself with liberating 160 pounds of silver. The British could not let him go on taunting them. But it was not until September 23 that they made a serious attempt to put him and his antiquated ship, *Bonhomme Richard*, out of commission.

REVOLUTIONARY REVELATIONS

On June 3, 1778, an embarrassed Jones told Benjamin Franklin that he was broke. He had spent £1,500 of his own money, but had not received any wages to offset his expenditure. Finally, on July 25, 1781, Congress approved his accounts and referred him to the Treasury Board for payment.

In one of the most famous battles in naval history, Jones captured and commandeered the British warship *Serapis*, which was escorting a British convoy carrying naval supplies to England. The *Serapis* was much larger than the *Bonhomme Richard* and outgunned it considerably. Jones used his expert seamanship skills to close in on the *Serapis*, tie the ships together, and negate the larger ship's firepower advantage. Eventually, Jones's crew prevailed, although he lost his ship. The *Bonhomme Richard* was damaged so badly it was no longer seaworthy. It sank between 10 and 11 A.M. on September 25, 1778. The victorious Jones and his crew sailed off aboard the *Serapis*—and into the annals of naval warfare history.

The battle ended Jones's fighting career with the U.S. navy. From that point on he was kept busy handling political and administrative affairs in Paris and receiving awards for his bravery and daring.

REVOLUTIONARY REVELATIONS

On July 21, 1778, the King of France received Jones at Versailles and presented him with a gold sword in recognition of his accomplishments on the behalf of independence.

Jones bounced around Europe for a couple years, and negotiated for prize money from Denmark. Then, the Russians asked him to join their navy.

He hoisted his flag as a rear admiral in the Russian navy aboard *Wolodimir* on May 26, 1788.

In mid-1788, Jones fought against the Turks and performed as brilliantly as he had for the American navy in the Revolutionary War. He left the Russian navy in mid-1789, planning to return to the United States to purchase a farm. It was 127 years before he made the trip.

Jones died in Paris on July 18, 1792, and was buried in a local cemetery. When it came time to exhume his remains and return him to the United States, no one could find his grave.

On July 14, 1848, the secretary of the U.S. Navy, William A. Graham, learned that the Protestant cemetery in the rear of the Hotel Dieu in Paris where Jones was supposed to have been buried had been sold. All the bones were removed to a different location.

Finally, on February 22, 1905, General Horace Porter, U.S. ambassador to France, announced that Jones's remains had been located. President Theodore Roosevelt dispatched a ship to bring John Paul Jones home. He was reburied at the United States Naval Academy in Annapolis, Maryland, at a ceremony in April 1906.

It had been a long trip, but the naval hero of the Revolutionary War was finally home.

If anyone sat down in the mid-1700s and drew up a list of top ten prospects for the Founding Fathers' roster, Rufus King might not have been considered among them. Yet, he completed law school, participated in the Revolutionary War, served in the Massachusetts legislature, the Confederation Congress and the U.S. Senate, and attended the federal Constitutional Convention in Philadelphia. And, in a political maneuver that history books don't cover, he established the precedent of moving from one state to another to earn election to the U.S. Senate. All that from a man whose father had fought for the British army in the French and Indian War and remained a Tory until he died! Rufus was as principled as his father—but on the opposite side.

A Promising Beginning

Rufus King graduated from Harvard in 1777 and began studying law under Theophilus Parsons, the man who convinced Samuel Adams and John Hancock to vote for ratification of the U.S. Constitution.

King took a break from his law studies to participate as a militiaman in the inconclusive Battle of Rhode Island on August 29, 1778. King served as an aide-de-camp to General John Sullivan in the skirmish, which was an unsuccessful American attempt to drive the British out of Newport, Rhode Island, which they had occupied since 1776. The British did not leave the city until October 1779, and even then they departed voluntarily.

After the battle ended, King returned to Boston, finished his law studies, and became a member of the state's bar. His star began to rise.

FEDERAL FACTS

The Battle of Rhode Island was the first incident in the Revolutionary War in which French forces took part.

Is the Republic Ready for Independence?

In 1783, King was elected to the Massachusetts General Court for the first of three terms. He also served in the Confederation Congress from 1784 to 1787, where he was the youngest member.

One of King's finest moments in the Congress occurred in 1784, when he supported a five-percent impost it asked from the states to fund its existence. The states did not have any desire to pay it, and Congress's efforts to collect the levy fell on deaf ears. King took their failure to fulfill their obligations as a personal affront. He was frustrated at every turn, but he worked hard to get all the states to grant the requested money. His efforts were a turning point in waking state governments to the fact that the federal government could not function without the states' contributions—financial and otherwise.

King worked hard for the ratification of the U.S. Constitution, first as a delegate to the federal convention in Philadelphia in 1787, then as a Massachusetts representative in its ratification proceedings. He was not always sure the people of the United States really cared one way or the other if the Constitution was ratified, but he worked tirelessly anyway.

King was not entirely altruistic. He hoped that Massachusetts would appoint him to the U.S. Senate. It did not—but New York did.

After Massachusetts elected Tristam Dalton as its first U.S. Senator, King, who had hoped to win the seat, invented a time-honored tactic.

King moved to another state that would elect him. In 1789, New York named him and Philip Schuyler as its first two U.S. Senators.

Quotations to Live (and Die) By!

"I MYSELF HAVE BEEN AN ADVOCATE FOR A GOVERN-
MENT FREE AS AIR; MY OPINIONS HAVE BEEN ESTAB-
LISHED UPON THE BELIEF, THAT MY COUNTRY MEN WERE
VIRTUOUS, ENLIGHTENED, AND GOVERNED BY A SENSE
OF RIGHT & WRONG. I HAVE EVER FEARED THAT IF
OUR REPUBLICAN GOVERNMENTS WERE SUBVERTED, IT
WOULD BE BY THE INFLUENCE OF COMMER[C]E AND THE
PROGRESS OF LUXURY."
—RUFUS KING

King served one full term in the U.S. Senate and was reelected in 1795, but President George Washington appointed him as the United States' ambassador to Britain in 1796. He remained in that post until 1803, when he asked President Thomas Jefferson to bring him home.

More Ups and Downs than an Elevator

King ran unsuccessfully as the Federalist Party's candidate for vice president in 1804 and 1808. He took a break from politics until 1813, when he was elected again to the U.S. Senate. He completed a six-year term, although he interrupted it to run for governor of New York and president of the United States in 1816. He lost both elections.

In the presidential election, James Monroe won 68.2 percent of the popular vote and 183 electoral votes, compared to King's 30.9 percent and 34 respectively. King had the honor of being the last presidential candidate to be nominated by the Federalist Party.

Undaunted, King returned to the U.S. Senate and won another reelection in 1820. He spent his final term in the Senate campaigning against slavery, which was becoming a hot issue.

After he left the Senate in 1825, King undertook a voyage to England at President John Quincy Adams's request to become the United States' ambassador to England. King completed a year in England, but his seventy years of activity were beginning to wear him down and he returned home, dying shortly thereafter. His distinguished record in public service showed that perhaps he should have been on that "Top Ten Prospects" list after all.

HENRY KNOX

Boston, Massachusetts
July 25, 1750 – October 25, 1806
Call in the "Big Guns"

Though most know Henry Knox as our nation's first secretary of war (and the namesake of the United States Army's famous Fort Knox), he was not always a professional soldier. In fact, before the Revolutionary War began, Knox's only claim to fame was being a successful bookseller in Boston. However, he turned a new page in his life when the fighting began by joining the militia as an artillery specialist. Knox eventually moved up through the ranks to become the Continental Army's chief artillery officer, where his crowning achievement was transporting the cannon that made the pivotal difference in the siege of Boston. Later in his life, he became one of the most controversial patriots of the Revolutionary War era.

Opportunity "Knox"

Although he'd been a quiet bookseller in Boston for four years, when the Revolutionary War began Knox quickly became involved in the fighting. He did not have an army commission at the time, yet he directed the American artillery at the Battle of Bunker Hill and helped General Artemas Ward develop fortifications around Boston. Later, Knox was appointed a colonel in the army's artillery regiment.

> ### REVOLUTIONARY REVELATIONS
> Knox abandoned his bookstore—which he had opened on July 29, 1771—when the war began. British army officers stole or destroyed its entire stock.

After British troops and Massachusetts patriots exchanged fire at Lexington and Concord on April 19, 1775, the New England Army, as it was called, established a ring around Boston to contain the British army in the city. George Washington came to Boston to direct the siege, which lasted for eleven months. He recognized that more cannons could help turn the tide in the patriots' favor. In May 1775, rebels led by Ethan Allen and Benedict Arnold had captured numerous cannons and other weapons at Fort Ticonderoga and Crown Point in New York, but they were 300 miles away. Washington couldn't just call a trucking firm to transport the guns to Boston. Knox said he would do the job. He did, despite the numerous obstacles in his way.

Knox relied on winter weather to transport the equipment between Ticonderoga and Boston, using ox-drawn sleds to do the job.

Knox had to hire workers and buy or rent animals along the route. Occasionally, guns broke through the ice and had to be retrieved. The journey took six weeks, instead of the two he had anticipated, but his tenacity paid off.

On January 25, 1776, Henry Knox reported to Washington in Boston with forty-five cannons and sixteen mortars. He and Washington placed them adroitly on Dorchester Heights, above the British troops. British General William Howe realized that the artillery put Washington at a distinct advantage. The "rumpus" Washington expected did not materialize because Howe and his troops left Boston and sailed to Nova Scotia. Knox and Washington, destined to become close friends and military leaders, departed to fight other battles. Washington took his troops to

New York. Knox helped set up defensive positions in Rhode Island and Connecticut before joining him there.

Quotations to Live (and Die) By!

"WE ARE PREPARING TO TAKE POSSESSION OF A POST WHICH WILL, IT IS GENERALLY THOUGHT, BRING ON A RUMPUS BETWEEN US AND THE ENEMY."

—GEORGE WASHINGTON, REGARDING DORCHESTER HEIGHTS

Crossing the Delaware

The Continental Army had a bad year in 1776. The British chased them from New York to New Jersey. Washington's raggedy army escaped the enemy by crossing the Delaware River on December 8, 1776. They had the foresight to seize all the boats along the river so the British could not follow them. The Americans did not stay on their side of the river for long, though. On Christmas night, they recrossed the river and captured 1,000 Hessian mercenaries fighting on the side of the British, along with their supplies. Knox directed the operation, which was a turning point in the war. It raised the troops' confidence and morale and bode badly for the British.

There were a few skirmishes after Christmas, during which Knox and his troops performed admirably. He earned a commendation from Washington for his exploits—but not a rest. In fact, he almost lost his position.

Silas Deane, the American minister to France, connived to have a French officer named Philippe Charles Tronson du Coudray (sometimes spelled Ducondray) replace Knox as Washington's chief artillery officer. He recruited du Coudray in France and sent him to General Washington with a recommendation that the Frenchman be appointed chief of artillery and the engineering corps. Du Coudray interviewed with Washington and then presented his credentials to Congress. Washington appealed to Congress and saved Knox's job. Congress compromised; on August 11, 1777, it appointed du Coudray to a position as an inspector general.

Washington's army crossed the Delaware River again and set up a winter camp at Morristown, New Jersey. Knox returned to Massachusetts to raise a battalion of troops and establish an arsenal at Springfield that proved valuable to the Americans for the rest of the war. Then his role changed. He became a fundraiser.

Show Me the Money

There was one thing Washington needed five years into war more than guns: money. He asked Knox to raise funds for him. Knox completed his mission successfully—and displayed his versatility once again.

In 1782 he was posted at West Point, where he remained until the British finally agreed to leave New York and the war ended. Knox then returned to Boston to continue his service to the United States.

An Unfortunate Demise

Congress appointed Knox to a position as secretary of war in 1785. He continued in that position until 1794, when he resigned due to the time-honored excuse of family obligations. His claim was not too far-fetched: Knox and his wife Lucy had thirteen children, of which only one survived to adulthood. And he was building a new house in Thomaston, Maine, to which he wanted to retire. The house was actually a mansion, and it created tension between Knox and the residents of Thomaston.

REVOLUTIONARY REVELATIONS

Washington offered Knox a position as a commissioner to St. Croix after he resigned as secretary of war, but Knox declined the assignment.

Quotations to Live (and Die) By!

"AFTER HAVING SERVED MY COUNTRY NEARLY TWENTY YEARS, THE GREATEST PORTION OF WHICH UNDER YOUR IMMEDIATE AUSPICES, IT IS WITH EXTREME RELUCTANCE, THAT I FIND MYSELF CONSTRAINED TO WITHDRAW FROM SO HONORABLE A STATION. BUT THE NATURAL AND POWERFUL CLAIMS OF A NUMEROUS FAMILY WILL NO LONGER PERMIT ME TO NEGLECT THEIR ESSENTIAL INTEREST. IN WHATEVER SITUATION I SHALL BE, I SHALL RECOLLECT YOUR CONFIDENCE AND KINDNESS WITH ALL THE POWER AND PURITY OF AFFECTION, OF WHICH A GRATEFUL HEART IS SUSCEPTIBLE."

—HENRY KNOX TO PRESIDENT WASHINGTON, DECEMBER 28, 1794

Knox and his family moved to Thomaston, Maine, in 1796, where he returned to his business roots. He dabbled in ventures such as brickmaking, cattle raising, shipbuilding, lumbering, and local politics. He served for a short while in the state's General Court and Governor's Council. Tragically, his life was cut short.

While visiting a friend on October 22, 1806, he swallowed a chicken bone, which led to an infection and his subsequent death.

Knox left behind an estate that was in dire financial arrears, a pile of debts, and a bad reputation among the local citizenry, who considered him a tyrant. Local people accused him of exploiting workers to enrich himself and of flaunting his wealth. They even threatened at one point to burn him out of what they felt was an ostentatious mansion.

But that did not detract from the fact that Henry Knox was one of the Revolutionary War era's unsung heroes.

ARTHUR LEE

Westmoreland County, Virginia
December 20, 1740–December 12, 1792
Provocateur Extraordinaire

Arthur Lee studied law in London and medicine in Edinburgh, Scotland, and practiced law in London for many years. Like his older brothers, Richard Henry and Francis Lightfoot, he was no great fan of British taxation policies in America. While he was in England he produced pamphlets and essays decrying his host country's slavery and anti-American policies, including his popular 1764 tract, *An Essay in Vindication of the Continental Colonies of America.* He took up the patriot cause when he got back to America, where he was well received at first. He wore out his welcome eventually. Arthur Lee was an example of patriots who supported independence, but all too often got in the way instead of helping.

A Spy in England's Midst

Arthur Lee, who was born and reared in Virginia, traveled to London (the date is unknown) to study law. While he was living in London, Congress authorized him to gather information on the feelings of European governments regarding the Americans' cause. Even then, government lived by poll results.

Although Lee had never set foot in Massachusetts, he represented the province in England. Consequently, Samuel Adams kept him apprised of events in Massachusetts.

Lee struck up a friendship with a French playwright named Pierre Augustin Caron, who wrote under the name of Beaumarchais. Caron was a secret agent for the French monarchy and arms supplier to the Americans during their rebellion. On June 12, 1775, Beaumarchais advised Lee in a letter that he was forming a company to "send help to your friend in the shape of powder and ammunition in exchange for tobacco."

Lee was in no position to do anything about procuring goods on behalf of his "friend," clearly the colonies, at the time. Besides, he was not a particularly skilled negotiator, as his record in soliciting foreign governments' aid proved.

Lee no sooner returned to the colonies in 1776 than he was asked to go back that same year to Europe, this time to France, as part of a diplomatic mission with Silas Deane and Ben Franklin.

REVOLUTIONARY REVELATIONS

Lee had met Franklin in London, where Lee vied for top billing as an envoy to the British government. He had no use for the older man. Lee suggested in a letter to Samuel Adams that Franklin was a philanderer who would never be a good negotiator between a free people and a tyrant.

Three Americans in Paris

Deane and Beaumarchais apparently worked out an arrangement regarding Beaumarchais's supplying materiel to the United States. Lee was under the impression, based on what Beaumarchais had told him in London, that the supplies were a gift. Deane was under the impression that they were part of a business deal that Congress was paying for with produce or money at some unspecified date. After the war, Beaumarchais insisted that the United States government owed him 3.6 million livres. (The franc did not become the official French currency until the French

Revolution occurred.) The government held back on payment after reviewing the receipts the American commission had given the French government. Discrepancies revealed the French had already paid Beaumarchais one million livres for the materiel.

After several reviews of the accounts, Lee claimed that Beaumarchais owed the United States 1.8 million livres, since he had already been paid by the French government. The convoluted situation led Lee to claim that Deane and Franklin were cooking the books in France, and at least one of them, Deane, was making a few livres of his own.

Because Lee suspected Deane of skullduggery and he just did not like Franklin, he notified Congress that they were not helping the Americans much. Deane did not have too high an opinion of Lee, either.

Just for good measure, Lee observed in his November 27, 1777, journal that Deane favored an alliance with Britain. Franklin, he noted, thought just the opposite.

Lee decided that removing Deane from the commission was in America's best interest.

Lee Completes His Service

Congress recalled Deane based on allegations of misconduct that Lee filed with them. John Adams arrived to replace Deane. He discovered quickly that nothing would get done unless he did it.

Quotations to Live (and Die) By!

"MY TWO COLLEAGUES WOULD AGREE ON NOTHING."
—JOHN ADAMS

Franklin could not be found most of the time, and Lee seldom arrived at the commission's office before 11 A.M. Somehow, they wrapped up the treaties with the French and Lee moved on.

Congress dissolved the commission in France late in 1778 and sent Lee to Madrid, where he negotiated unsuccessfully for help from the Spanish.

Meanwhile, in Philadelphia, the furor over the Deane affair and gossip about the hatred between Franklin and Lee tarnished Lee's reputation at home and abroad.

Eventually, Lee returned to the United States and a hostile reception from Congress, which had separated into quarreling factions as a result of the Deane debacle. Lee returned to Virginia in 1780, where he served in the Virginia General Assembly, in 1781–83, 1785, and 1786, and as a member of the Continental Congress in 1782–84. (The House of Burgesses was renamed the Virginia General Assembly in 1776.) He completed his government service from 1784–89, when he served as a Treasury board official.

FEDERAL FACTS

Lee was never one to support something he did not believe in. In his last term in Congress, he found himself on the wrong side of a national argument. He opposed the federal Constitution because he thought it would create an oligarchy (a small group of people, usually wealthy ones) and because it lacked a bill of rights.

Being on the wrong side of an issue did not bother Lee. He simply wanted to serve his government, opposing views notwithstanding.

Finally, Lee, disillusioned and embittered, went home to Virginia to live out his final years. He outlived Deane and Franklin, but he could not outlive the damage to his reputation that he incurred due to his personal differences with them. His heart had been in the right place, but it overruled his head. Arthur Lee was proof that good intentions did not always lead to good results, but he supported his country nonetheless.

RICHARD HENRY LEE

Westmoreland County, Virginia
January 20, 1732 – June 19, 1794
An Underappreciated Radical

Richard H. Lee was one of the first to say out loud what most of the delegates to the Second Continental Congress were thinking: Let us seek independence from Britain and form our own country. Years later, he wrote the Tenth Amendment to the U.S. Constitution to protect states' rights under a federal government. He did not always say a lot in the legislative bodies in which he served, but when he did speak or write, the results were meaningful—and are still being felt today. Yet history books seldom assign significant importance to his contributions to the patriots' cause.

Silent Lee

As a young man, Richard Henry Lee attended a private school in England, and then stayed in Europe for a couple years after he finished his studies. He did not show much interest in a profession when he returned to Virginia in 1751, being content to stay around the family plantation and dabble in whatever interested him. But he could not lead a life of leisure forever.

A few years after Lee returned to Virginia, the French and Indian War broke out. He organized a group of young men living in his neighborhood into a militia troop and they elected him the leader of the pack. The militia marched off to Alexandria, Virginia, to offer their service to

General Edward Braddock, who was preparing for a campaign on the Ohio River. Braddock said "No, thanks" and sent them home. That ended Lee's military career.

 Quotations to Live (and Die) By!

"TO PRESERVE LIBERTY IT IS ESSENTIAL THAT THE WHOLE BODY OF PEOPLE ALWAYS POSSESS ARMS AND BE TAUGHT ALIKE, ESPECIALLY WHEN YOUNG, HOW TO USE THEM."

—RICHARD HENRY LEE

However, his political career was just beginning. The people of Westmoreland County were not willing to let a good Lee go to waste. He was appointed to a position as justice of the peace in 1757. Lee was also elected to the Virginia House of Burgesses that year. He did not leave the House until 1775.

Listen, Learn—and Then Act

Lee did not impress anybody at the House of Burgesses right away. He was standoffish and quiet. Lee occasionally displayed strong oratorical skills, but it was a few years before he got involved fully in the Burgesses' businesses. Once he did, there was no holding him back.

When Patrick Henry introduced his resolves against the Stamp Act in 1765, Lee supported them vigorously. As opposition to Britain's increasing tax levies on the colonies grew in the mid-1700s, Lee became more outspoken. By 1774, he felt the time for talking had ended. He wanted independence.

In 1774 Virginia's Royal Governor Lord Dunmore dissolved the House of Burgesses that met in Williamsburg. That displeased a group of radical members of the House. They moved to the nearby Raleigh Tavern and began planning their next step. The sometimes diffident Richard Lee was among them.

Lee was elected to the First Continental Congress in 1774. He had an advantage over other congressional members, since his brother William—an American spy who was living in England, serving as the sheriff of London, and campaigning for a seat in Parliament—told him what Britain planned to do.

At the Second Continental Congress in Philadelphia, Lee introduced motions for independence, foreign alliances, and a union of American states on June 7, 1776. Very few people know that it was he, not Thomas Jefferson, who authored the resolution.

 Quotations to Live (and Die) By!

"RESOLVED, THAT THESE UNITED COLONIES ARE, AND OF RIGHT OUGHT TO BE, FREE AND INDEPENDENT STATES, THAT THEY ARE ABSOLVED FROM ALL ALLE-GIANCE TO THE BRITISH CROWN, AND THAT ALL POLITI-CAL CONNECTION BETWEEN THEM AND THE STATE OF GREAT BRITAIN IS, AND OUGHT TO BE TOTALLY DIS-SOLVED . . ."

—RICHARD LEE'S RESOLUTION FOR INDEPENDENCE AT THE SECOND CONTINENTAL CONGRESS

Shortly thereafter, the Congress began discussions about his resolution, which included two other parts: a call to form foreign alliances and a call to submit a plan of confederation for ratification by the colonies. The members followed his advice, which led to the signing of the Declaration of Independence two months later. Lee's work was almost done.

Not a Washington Fan

Lee served in Congress during the Revolutionary War. At one point he locked horns with George Washington over his military leadership, especially after the Battles of Brandywine and Germantown in Pennsylvania, in which the American troops performed poorly. Lee was also critical of Silas Deane and Benjamin Franklin for their alleged mishandling of foreign affairs.

FEDERAL FACTS

Richard Lee's brother, Francis Lightfoot, also signed the Declaration of Independence.

Washington was not pleased with the criticism, especially from a fellow Virginian. The affair blew over, and Washington and Lee moved on.

Quotations to Live (and Die) By!

"To Sum up the whole, I have been a Slave to the service: I have undergone more than most Men are aware of, to harmonize so many discordant parts; but it will be impossible for me to be of any further service, if such insuperable difficulties are thrown in my way."

—George Washington in an October 17, 1777, letter to Richard Henry Lee

Preserving States' Rights

Lee continued to serve in the Virginia House of Burgesses and the Continental Congress after the war ended. If there was one thing Richard Henry Lee was adamant about, it was states' rights over a strong federal government. Consequently, he was concerned that the new U.S. Constitution being written in the late 1780s would favor a strong federal government.

As a U.S. senator (elected in 1789), he wanted to ensure that the individual states reserved at least some rights. Therefore, he wrote an amendment to the U.S. Constitution, one of ten that became collectively known as the Bill of Rights. The Tenth Amendment was his final big moment on the political stage. The Bill of Rights was adopted by the House of Representatives on August 21, 1789. Lee retired from the Senate three years later because of ill health.

Quotations to Live (and Die) By!

"THE POWERS NOT DELEGATED TO THE UNITED STATES BY THE CONSTITUTION, NOR PROHIBITED BY IT TO THE STATES, ARE RESERVED TO THE STATES RESPECTIVELY, OR TO THE PEOPLE."

—TENTH AMENDMENT TO THE U.S. CONSTITUTION

REVOLUTIONARY REVELATIONS

Richard Henry Lee was Confederate Civil War General Robert E. Lee's grandfather.

Richard Henry Lee completed his journey from diffidence to resolution in 1794; two of his resolutions, years apart, had a significant impact on the history of the United States.

PHILIP LIVINGSTON

Albany, New York
January 15, 1716–June 12, 1778
Supreme Sacrifice Too Soon

Most of the signers of the Declaration of Independence lived to see what they had wrought. Philip Livingston, a successful New York merchant and politician, was one of the few who did not. Livingston experienced a lot of welcome and unwelcome political changes in his lifetime, but he never got to see the independent United States he had envisioned. He epitomized the family relationships that were so prominent in the Revolutionary era. Philip was one of three Livingstons who were members of the Continental Congress, although he was the only one who signed the Declaration. The others were his brother William and his first cousin once removed Robert L. Livingston.

From Albany to Philadelphia via New York City

Philip Livingston graduated from Yale in 1737, before some of the signers of the Declaration of Independence were born. He owned a house in Manhattan, a forty-acre farm in Brooklyn Heights, and a home in Albany. He also maintained a residence in Kingston, New York, where his family moved to escape the British army when it occupied New York City. Livingston's first political position was assistant alderman in Albany. He held the position in 1743, 1744, and 1745. After completing his political apprenticeship in Albany, he moved to New York City to enter the import business. He became an alderman there in 1754, and held the post for nine years. His next step was the New York Provincial Assembly, where he served from 1759–68. He was highly critical of British tax policies, which directly affected his life as a merchant. Livingston, like so many of his contemporaries, was not against taxes or British governance per se. He just did not like taxation without representation, and acted to stop the practice.

Quotations to Live (and Die) By!

"DEPRESSED WITH THIS PROSPECT OF INEVITABLE RUIN . . .
WHICH, IF CARRIED INTO EXECUTION, WILL OBLIGE US
TO THINK THAT NOTHING BUT EXTREME POVERTY CAN
PRESERVE US FROM THE MOST INSUPPORTABLE BONDAGE.
WE HOPE YOUR HONOR [THE LIEUTENANT GOVERNOR
OF NEW YORK] WILL JOIN WITH US IN AN ENDEAVOR TO
SECURE THAT GREAT BADGE OF ENGLISH LIBERTY, OF
BEING TAXED ONLY WITH OUR OWN CONSENT . . ."
—PHILIP LIVINGSTON

Livingston moonlighted as a political activist in New York City while he served in the colony's Provincial Assembly by participating as a member of several local resistance committees.

When the Continental Army was mulling a withdrawal from New York City to New Jersey in 1776, officers met at Livingston's house on August 29 to discuss their strategy.

The patriots of New York recognized his dedication to their cause. In 1774, Livingston was elected to the First Continental Congress. As a delegate to the Second Continental Congress in 1776, he signed the Declaration of Independence. Livingston was one of the oldest signers.

Quotations to Live (and Die) By!

"MR. LIVINGSTON IS A DOWNRIGHT, STRAIGHTFORWARD MAN."

—JOHN ADAMS

A Change of Venue

The New York Assembly sent Livingston back to the Continental Congress in 1777 and 1778. In New York, the state was writing its own constitution and Livingston attended the meeting convened to draft the document, which was adopted in Kingston, New York, on April 20, 1777. A month later, Livingston was elected to the state Senate convened under the auspices of the new constitution. He represented the southern district.

In October 1777, the New York Senate elected representatives to the Continental Congress. By that time, it had become a habit to elect Livingston. Sure enough, he received an appointment to the 1778 Continental Congress. By the time the Congress convened in May, the British army had taken possession of Philadelphia, where the Congress usually met. The venue was changed to York, ninety-five miles west of Philadelphia.

REVOLUTIONARY REVELATIONS

Philip Livingston was experiencing health problems in the late 1770s. He was suffering from "dropsy," the quaint term used at the time to describe the swelling of soft tissues due to the accumulation of excess water.

The Final Sacrifice

Philip Livingston knew he was dying, and that there was very little chance that he would recover from his illness. He could have stayed at home and died in peace with his loved ones at his side. That was not in his plans. He made a tour of New York state to say his final goodbyes.

First, he visited Albany to wish his friends farewell. Next, he traveled to Kingston to say goodbye to his family. Only then did he undergo the arduous trek to York.

Livingston's health went downhill as soon as he reached York. Thirty-eight days after he started his duties with the Congress, he died. Congress observed Philip Livingston's passing with a month of mourning.

The true tragedy of Livingston's death was the fact that he did not live to see the aftermath of the signing of the Declaration of Independence. However, those who did thanked Philip Livingston, who dedicated his life to make sure his successors lived in freedom.

ROBERT R. LIVINGSTON

New York, New York
November 27, 1746–February 26, 1813
Mr. Eclectic

Robert Livingston was like a comic book hero. He showed up when he was needed, helped save the day, and retreated into history. He served with the Provincial Congress of New York and the Continental Congress, participated in New York state's U.S. Constitution ratification process, spent a few years as the country's minister to the court of Napoleon, returned to New York, and tinkered with sheep and steamboats. He packed a lot of accomplishments into a short career, which was exactly what the people of the United States needed at the time.

Throw Away the Carbon Copy

The resumes of young New York gentlemen in the mid-1700s, including Robert R. Livingston's, could have been printed on a standard form. All they had to do was fill in their names and birth dates. From that point on, the form would have read "Born, studied at King's College, passed the bar exam, worked at or opened a law practice . . ."

The passage of the Stamp Act changed that rubber stamp form for many of them—especially Robert R. Livingston.

Robert Livingston and his brother William were suspected of being active with the Sons of Liberty in New York in the era of the Stamp Act revolt. Most of the Sons were not eager to reveal their identities for fear of retribution. In fact, Robert lost his job as a recorder of the city of New

York in 1775 because of his anti-British sympathies—but in that same year he was elected to the New York Provincial Congress. That body, in turn, sent him to the Second Continental Congress.

REVOLUTIONARY REVELATIONS

Robert R. Livingston was John Jay's classmate at King's College. He and Jay worked together in a law partnership for a short time after they graduated.

There was no doubt that Livingston believed that a split between the colonies and Britain was inevitable, but he was not prepared to advocate independence when he first arrived in Philadelphia.

Quotations to Live (and Die) By!

"IT WAS ARGUED BY WILSON, ROBERT R. LIVINGSTON, E. RUTLEDGE, DICKINSON AND OTHERS: THAT THO' THEY WERE FRIENDS TO THE [INDEPENDENCE] MEASURES THEMSELVES, AND SAW THE IMPOSSIBILITY THAT WE SHOULD EVER AGAIN BE UNITED WITH GR. BRITAIN, YET THEY WERE AGAINST ADOPTING THEM AT THIS TIME."

—THOMAS JEFFERSON, "NOTES OF PROCEEDINGS IN THE CONTINENTAL CONGRESS"

Nevertheless, Livingston was appointed to a five-person committee responsible for preparing a draft of the Declaration of Independence. The committee turned the job over to Jefferson, who completed the draft ultimately signed by fifty-six members of the Congress. Livingston was not among them—but not because he was opposed to it.

New York's Provincial Assembly had recalled Robert R. Livingston to vote on a name change from "province" to "state." Livingston left Philadelphia early in July to work on the name change and help a committee draft a new state constitution. As a result, he was not in Philadelphia on August 2, 1776, to sign the Declaration of Independence.

Holding Down Two Jobs

New York state adopted its new constitution in 1777. The delegates named Livingston the state's first chancellor (governor) in conformance with the new document.

He retained that position until 1801. Livingston also continued to serve in the Continental Congress during 1777 and 1779–81. He was constantly involved in and apprised of war-related activities that might affect his state.

REVOLUTIONARY REVELATIONS

As chancellor of New York, Robert R. Livingston administered the oath of office to the first president of the United States, George Washington. He concluded his participation with the words, "Long live George Washington, president of the United States."

From 1781–83, Livingston served as the country's secretary of foreign affairs and participated in the peace talks with the French government in an effort to draft a treaty to end the war. There were few events of historical significance in the next twenty years in which Livingston was not involved.

He chaired New York's U.S. Constitution ratification committee in 1788. But he was not comfortable with federal positions because they conflicted with his duties as chancellor. He turned down assignments as minister to France and secretary of the navy in the 1790s.

Finally, he gave in. The fact that he had to give up his chancellor's position due to state constitutional limitations probably had something to do with it, but Livingston accepted President Thomas Jefferson's offer to serve as his minister to France. It was a wise selection by Jefferson.

Livingston was instrumental in coordinating the Louisiana Purchase in 1803 and easing the tension between France and the United States that had resulted in their 1798–1800 Quasi-War. Livingston decided by 1804 that he had done enough for his country and opted to end his public service career.

FEDERAL FACTS

Napoleon Bonaparte, the emperor of France, was fond of Robert Livingston. As a farewell gift Bonaparte gave Livingston a fancy snuff box and a heartwarming adieu.

Letting Off Steam

After close to forty years of public service, Livingston was ready to pursue his numerous and varied hobbies. While he was in Paris, Livingston met Robert Fulton, who is considered to be the inventor of the steamboat. He probably could not have done it without Livingston. The two worked together in France to develop a boat that would travel at least three to four miles per hour. They made a few trial runs on the Seine River, but did not build a steamship that was capable of reaching a high speed until they got back to New York. Finally, in 1807, they built the *Clermont*, named after Livingston's estate. The boat attained the blazing speed of seven miles per hour.

Livingston also became involved in scientific and farming interests after he returned to the United States. He spent a good part of his free time experimenting with agricultural methods, raising merino sheep, and serving on the boards of the American Academy of Fine Arts and the New York Society Library.

The comic book–like hero turned his last page in 1813 and steamed into history, leaving behind a significant list of accomplishments.

JAMES MADISON

Port Conway, Virginia
March 16, 1751 – June 28, 1836
Putting Theory Into Practice

If James Madison were a professor at the university in Harrisonburg, Virginia, named after him, he could be the sole faculty member in the history and political science departments based on his experience and academic background. He had one of the longest careers among the Founding Fathers, holding positions from U.S. congressman to secretary of state and U.S. president. He was the "Father of the U.S. Constitution," the author of several "Federalist Papers," and the chief architect of the Bill of Rights. When something needed doing during the United States' formative years, the cry went out for Madison. He almost always delivered.

The Education of a Patriot

While most wealthy young Virginians who attended college in the mid-1700s attended the College of William & Mary, James Madison opted for Princeton College in New Jersey. His undergraduate and graduate course load at Princeton included Latin, Greek, Hebrew, science, geography, mathematics, rhetoric, philosophy, speech and debate, and political philosophy. He studied law after he graduated, but had no intention of becoming a practicing attorney. Madison believed wholeheartedly in the connection between the value of a good education and an enlightened society. It certainly paid off for him.

Quotations to Live (and Die) By!

"LEARNED INSTITUTIONS OUGHT TO BE FAVORITE
OBJECTS WITH EVERY FREE PEOPLE. THEY THROW THAT
LIGHT OVER THE PUBLIC MIND WHICH IS THE BEST
SECURITY AGAINST CRAFTY AND DANGEROUS ENCROACH-
MENTS ON THE PUBLIC LIBERTY."
—JAMES MADISON

Despite his desire to pursue a profession other than the law after returning to Virginia, Madison got involved in legal matters, especially those that involved religion.

At the time, non-Anglican ministers had to obtain licenses from the state church (the Church of England) to preach. Those who did not were subject to arrest.

Madison adopted religious freedom as a cause and worked closely with local preachers for the passage of laws regarding religious freedom. In 1774, he became a member of the Committee of Safety, whose purpose was to oversee the militia. Then he served in the Virginia House of Burgesses from 1776–1779 and 1784–86, where he and Thomas Jefferson became friends. That helped his career.

Madison was appointed in 1778 to the Virginia Council of State, which directed the state's affairs during the Revolutionary War. And he was a delegate to the Confederation Congress from Virginia from March 1781 to November 1783.

Although Madison did not serve in the Revolutionary War, he worked diligently behind the scenes for the cause of independence. One of his main concerns was finding the funds to finance the Revolutionary War. Once the war ended, Madison's political career took off.

Quotations to Live (and Die) By!

"The vicissitudes which our finances have under-gone are as great as those of the war."
    —James Madison

From Delicate Health to a Strong Constitution

Madison bounced back and forth from state to local politics in the 1780s.

While in the Virginia legislature, Madison helped write a religious free-dom statute that mitigated the state's ability to regulate religious matters. He argued against a plan espoused by Patrick Henry to force Virginians to "donate" money to a church of their choice to support the poor. He and Jef-ferson called Henry's suggested donation a tax. Their argument prevailed.

When the states were trying to write and ratify a national constitu-tion, Madison took a leading role.

Quotations to Live (and Die) By!

"What is government itself but the greatest of all reflections on human nature? If men were angels, no government would be necessary. If angels were to govern men, neither external nor internal controls on government would be necessary."
    —James Madison

Madison was a significant contributor in the writing of the U.S. Con-stitution and the Bill of Rights. He also wrote a large number of the "Federalist Papers" in support of their passage, in conjunction with Alex-ander Hamilton and John Jay. The Constitution and Bill of Rights were ultimately ratified.

After George Washington became president, he adopted the Federalists' philosophy of a strong central government that favored commercial and financial interests over agrarian interests. Madison and Jefferson separated themselves from Washington's party and formed their own, the Democratic-Republicans, to oppose him. Their chief fear was that the Federalists' financial proposals created by Alexander Hamilton and backed by Washington would make northern financiers wealthy and do little economically for southern agrarian-based interests.

President Madison

Thomas Jefferson appointed Madison as his secretary of state in 1801. He remained in that post for eight years, weathering some serious storms. The period was a difficult time for the United States, as the country tried to stay neutral in the ongoing wars between Britain and France and was engaged in a war with several North African countries (the Barbary States) over piracy and extortion. At the same time, British and French naval commanders made a habit of seizing American merchant ships and their cargoes at sea and impressing crew members into their services. The acts were a public relations nightmare for Madison, who could do little to stop the indignities due to the lack of a powerful U.S. navy. Americans were unhappy with Jefferson and Madison as a result. Ultimately, their unhappiness worked to Madison's advantage.

FEDERAL FACTS

The Barbary States exacted tributes from American merchant ships sailing near their territories in the Mediterranean Sea. To collect them, they often seized the vessels and held them and their crews for ransom. Jefferson and Madison deployed U.S. navy warships to confront them in what became a four-year war (1801–05). The Americans convinced the Barbary States that they might want to rethink their strategy, although the navy had to return in 1815 to finish the war.

Madison succeeded Jefferson as president in 1809. Within three years, the United States was in a war with Britain that neither country wanted. The chief causes were an 1810 ban on trade with Britain imposed by Madison and Britain's refusal to stop impounding American merchant ships, cargoes, and crew members. American "war hawks" in Congress, specifically Henry Clay and John C. Calhoun, pressed Madison to declare war on Britain. He acceded to their demands; Congress declared war on Britain on June 1, 1812. The two countries fought to a stalemate in what became known derisively in some regions, particularly New England, as "Mr. Madison's War."

Many Americans blamed Madison for the war, citing his inability or unwillingness to solve the issues between the two countries diplomatically. For the most part, American military forces had not performed well against the overwhelming might of the British army and navy. The nation had even suffered a major indignity in 1814 when British troops entered Washington, D.C., and set fire to the White House and the Capitol building. But American forces did earn a few significant military milestones against the British, such as Commodore Oliver Hazard Perry's September 10, 1813, naval victory on Lake Erie and General Andrew Jackson's January 8, 1815, triumph at New Orleans. These events instilled a renewed sense of nationalism and patriotic fervor in Americans, which led to a second term for Madison. Despite the charges that he had led the country into a needless conflict for which its military was not ready, Madison won reelection and had a less contentious second term.

REVOLUTIONARY REVELATIONS

James Madison is the only U.S. president under whom two vice presidents died while in office. George Clinton died on April 20, 1812, and Elbridge Gerry emulated him on November 23, 1814.

A Sedentary Life—and Death

Once the war ended, Madison returned to his Virginia plantation and a life of leisure. He succeeded Thomas Jefferson as head of the University of Virginia in 1826 and served as a delegate to the Virginia Constitutional Convention in 1829.

Mostly, though, he spent time with his popular wife, Dolley, whom he had married on September 15, 1794.

James Madison passed away peacefully at breakfast one summer morning after a six-month bout of bad health.

He left behind a legacy as one of the most influential Founding Fathers, and gratitude galore from the country for which he had done so much.

JOHN MARSHALL

Fauquier County, Virginia
September 24, 1755–July 6, 1835
Late Bloomer

John Marshall did not make a name for himself until after the Revolutionary War. He served in the Continental Army for several years, including the notorious winter at Valley Forge, Pennsylvania. Marshall resigned from the army in 1781 to study law. After that he held a number of political and judicial offices, including chief justice of the United States Supreme Court. In that capacity he changed the relationships among the three branches of government and between the federal and state governments. That, more than anything else he accomplished, is his legacy.

Winning Is Not Always a Good Thing

John Marshall began his law career with a capable mentor: He studied under George Wythe, one of Virginia's leading eighteenth-century lawyers. Marshall quickly acquired a reputation for integrity and political acumen that led to his success as a legislator and judge.

He began his political career by serving one term in the Virginia General Assembly, representing Fauquier County. Later, he served on the Council of State from 1782 to 1784. Immediately thereafter, Marshall returned to the Virginia Assembly. This time, he represented Henrico County, from 1784 to 1787. He also served in June of 1788 as a delegate to the Virginia state convention assembled to ratify the U.S. Constitution.

REVOLUTIONARY REVELATIONS

John Marshall was a talented quoits player, which was one of his favorite pastimes. The game involved throwing a metal ring over an iron stake embedded in the ground. He was a member of the exclusive Buchanan Spring Quoits Club, where political discussions were forbidden—but consuming a punch diluted with brandy, rum, and Madeira wine was encouraged. He was also good at that.

Political opportunities were limited in Fauquier County, so Marshall moved to Richmond, Virginia, in 1785. He plunged into local politics, albeit unsuccessfully at first. He ran for the city council, but placed second. That turned out to be a blessing in disguise. The runner-up prize was a position as city recorder. That served him in good stead in his legal career.

The city recorder's duty was to sit as a magistrate on a local court that handled minor civil and criminal cases. The position was a steppingstone for Marshall to higher court positions.

The experience in the Richmond court earned him a reputation that would follow him for the rest of his legal career. He was known as a man who adhered rigidly to three principles: subordinating self-interest to the public good, controlling oneself by reason, and maintaining a sense of duty.

Quotations to Live (and Die) By!

"THE PEOPLE MADE THE CONSTITUTION, AND THE PEO-PLE CAN UNMAKE IT. IT IS THE CREATURE OF THEIR OWN WILL, AND LIVES ONLY BY THEIR WILL."
—JOHN MARSHALL

Working His Way Up

Marshall combined his judicial and political responsibilities through-out the late 1700s. He served in the Virginia Assembly from 1782–91 and 1795–97. His accomplishments as a lawyer and judge over that time caught President George Washington's attention. Washington offered Marshall two positions: attorney general and minister to France in the mid-1790s. He declined both in favor of something bigger. Marshall's break came in 1800, when President John Adams named him as secretary of state.

REVOLUTIONARY REVELATIONS

John Marshall wrote a 3,200-page biography of George Washington that took him five years to complete. It sold 7,000 copies.

Marshall served as secretary of state from June 13, 1800, to March 13, 1801. On January 20, 1801, the outgoing president nominated him as chief justice of the Supreme Court. Marshall did not step down for thirty-four years. He was the longest-serving Supreme Court justice in U.S. history.

Chief Justice Marshall

Marshall made a major difference during his lengthy stint as the chief justice. Among his most significant accomplishments: he established the principle of judicial review, ruled that state judiciaries could set aside state legislative acts if they conflicted with the federal Constitution, and said that the U.S. Supreme Court could reverse a decision of a state court. He did note, however, that the powers of government were limited.

The cumulative effect of the three rulings was to increase the power of the Supreme Court as a branch of the federal government, emphasize the role of the judiciary in the states, and reinforce the national supremacy of the federal government.

 Quotations to Live (and Die) By!

"IT IS EMPHATICALLY THE PROVINCE AND DUTY OF THE JUDICIAL DEPARTMENT TO SAY WHAT THE LAW IS. . . . IF TWO LAWS CONFLICT WITH EACH OTHER, THE COURTS MUST DECIDE ON THE OPERATION OF EACH. . . . THIS IS OF THE VERY ESSENCE OF JUDICIAL DUTY."
—JOHN MARSHALL

Amazingly, even though Marshall served on the Supreme Court for thirty-four years, he did not render many significantly controversial rulings. One of the few that stood out, Marbury v. Madison (1803), set a precedent that affects the way the federal government operates today.

Marbury v. Madison involved a refusal by President Jefferson's secretary of state, James Madison, to deliver William Marbury's commission as a justice of the peace in Washington, D.C. Marbury asked the court to compel the government to grant his commission. The Supreme Court justices ruled that he was entitled to the commissions. But they said the Judiciary Act of 1789, which had given the court the power to grant it, was inconsistent with the U.S. Constitution. Therefore, they declared, the act was invalid.

The ruling made the Supreme Court the final decision maker regarding the constitutionality of congressional legislation.

In another well-known case, the Supreme Court under Marshall exonerated Aaron Burr of treason, after a June 24, 1807, indictment on charges that he had instigated a war against Spain. The case stemmed from a bizarre incident which then President Thomas Jefferson knew nothing about, even though it could have led the United States into a war.

In 1805 Burr had held secret meetings with Brigadier General James Wilkinson, governor of the Louisiana Territory, commander of the U.S. Army, and a secret agent of the Spanish Crown, regarding the purchase of one million acres of land in the south on which Burr would build his own empire.

Just who owned the land was in question. Spain claimed part of it, and threatened to go to war with the United States over the issue. Another chunk of the land would be taken from Mexico. Wilkinson agreed to supply U.S. troops for the invasion as part of the scheme. The plan unraveled when Wilkinson advised President Jefferson of what was happening. Burr was captured and charged with treason.

The case reached the Supreme Court, which ruled that Burr may have been guilty of something, but it was not treason. The man who had killed Alexander Hamilton in a duel walked free. He never did set up his own empire.

Marshall walked a tightrope in his years as chief justice. He consistently ruled fairly and impartially, and set judicial precedents that the Supreme Court is still following two centuries later.

JAMES MONROE

Westmoreland County, Virginia
April 28, 1758–July 4, 1831
The Birth of NIMBY-ism

James Monroe fought in the Revolutionary War and served as the U.S. ambassador to France and Great Britain, a U.S. senator, secretary of state and war, and fifth U.S. president. He developed the Monroe Doctrine and helped negotiate the Louisiana Purchase. There were very few events of significance in which he did not participate in the United States' first fifty years. Monroe was one of the country's early political stars and his legacy is still felt today.

It's Who You Know

James Monroe entered the College of William & Mary at age sixteen, but left shortly thereafter to fight in the Revolutionary War with the Third Virginia Regiment. Actually, his fight against the British began before he left the campus, as he participated in rebellious activities around Williamsburg that surpassed the normal student pranks. James Monroe and a few classmates raided the arsenal at the British governor's palace in Williamsburg. They captured 200 muskets and 300 swords, which they turned over to the Virginia militia. Not many of the Founding Fathers carried out "pranks" of that magnitude.

The young lieutenant managed to be where the fighting took place early in the war. He fought at Harlem Heights, White Plains, Trenton, Brandywine, Germantown, and Monmouth. He was one of five American casualties at the Battle of Trenton in December 1776. A musket ball struck Monroe in the left shoulder and severed an artery. A New Jersey physician named Dr. John Riker clamped the artery quickly enough to stop the bleeding—and save the future president's life.

Eventually, he rose to the rank of lieutenant colonel owing to General Washington's influence, but he left the army in 1780 to pursue his law studies.

Monroe had an uncanny knack for befriending illustrious political figures. In addition to drawing George Washington's attention during the Revolutionary War, he studied law under Thomas Jefferson's tutelage. Their relationship evolved into a lifetime friendship, which helped Monroe ascend the political ladder.

Those connections benefited him as his career progressed and he fulfilled his desire to build a stronger United States.

 Quotations to Live (and Die) By!

"NEVER DID A GOVERNMENT COMMENCE UNDER AUSPICES SO FAVORABLE, NOR EVER WAS SUCCESS SO COMPLETE. IF WE LOOK TO THE HISTORY OF OTHER NATIONS, ANCIENT OR MODERN, WE FIND NO EXAMPLE OF A GROWTH SO RAPID, SO GIGANTIC, OF A PEOPLE SO PROSPEROUS AND HAPPY."

—JAMES MONROE

A Meteoric Rise

Monroe got into politics soon after he finished law school. He was elected to the Virginia House of Delegates in 1782 and was appointed to Governor's Council. Monroe also served in the Congress of the Confederation from 1783–86.

Monroe made a name for himself in Congress by insisting on the United States' right to navigate the Mississippi River and attempting to enforce Congress's power to regulate commerce. He did not have much success in either endeavor, so he resigned and set up his own law practice in Fredericksburg, Virginia. His retirement from politics did not last long, as his fellow Virginians demanded his services, in and out of the state.

FEDERAL FACTS

The Confederation Congress (a.k.a. the United States in Congress Assembled) was one of the names for the U.S. Congress that convened from March 1, 1781, to March 4, 1789.

Quotations to Live (and Die) By!

"OUR COUNTRY MAY BE LIKENED TO A NEW HOUSE. WE LACK MANY THINGS, BUT WE POSSESS THE MOST PRECIOUS OF ALL—LIBERTY!"

—JAMES MONROE

Monroe was a member of the Virginia House of Delegates in 1787. A year later he became a member of the Virginia convention that ratified the federal constitution. Then, he was appointed in 1790 to fill the Senate vacancy caused by the death of William Grayson. To add to his accomplishments, he received a nomination from President Washington on May 27, 1794, as ambassador to France. It may be that Washington simply wanted to get Monroe out of the country—during his term as senator, Monroe consistently opposed Washington's government.

President Monroe

Monroe returned to Virginia to serve as governor from 1799–1802. President Jefferson enlisted his aid in 1803 to help negotiate the Louisiana Purchase. Subsequently, Jefferson nominated him to the post of ambassador to England.

Monroe's tenure in England was a trying time for the young United States. The two countries were arguing over the British navy's policy of impressing (i.e., forcing to serve) American seamen to act as crewmen on its ships. Monroe tried unsuccessfully to negotiate a treaty to stop the practice.

Jefferson recalled Monroe in 1807. It was one of the few failures in Monroe's political career.

REVOLUTIONARY REVELATIONS

James Monroe was the only person to serve as both secretary of war and secretary of state at the same time. He held both positions during the War of 1812.

Finally, in 1816, he was elected to the first of his two terms as U.S. president.

Several major events took place on Monroe's watch. Among the most significant were the 1817–18 war with the Seminole Indians, the acquisition of Florida from Spain, and the Missouri Compromise.

The Missouri Compromise addressed the constitutional conflict over the existence of slavery in the United States. According to the terms, after 1820, states above the southern Missouri border would be slavefree. Those below could be slave states. In reality, the compromise just highlighted the sectional divisions in the country that future generations were left to resolve.

The Monroe Doctrine

The best known legacy of Monroe's presidency is the Monroe Doctrine. It is still invoked today—even though the man it's named after has been dead for almost 200 years.

The Monroe Doctrine announced on December 2, 1823, was clear and concise. It warned European powers planning on interfering in the United States' sphere of influence in the Western Hemisphere to think twice before acting, lest they bear the full brunt of its political and military power—not that the United States possessed much of either at the time. Monroe's "doctrine," as it came to be known years later, was a radical departure for a government that had attained its own independence only forty-seven years earlier. It marked the first time that the United States flexed its muscles regarding the Western Hemisphere, and signaled that the former British colonies had "grown up." In effect, he was acknowledging that the political system in the Western Hemisphere was more like the United States' than Europe's. The imposition of the doctrine capped Monroe's significant political career—and was a major milestone for the Founding Fathers.

 Quotations to Live (and Die) By!

"THE BEST FORM OF GOVERNMENT IS THAT WHICH IS MOST LIKELY TO PREVENT THE GREATEST SUM OF EVIL."
—JAMES MONROE

While Monroe was visiting his daughter Maria in New York City in 1831, he died—on Independence Day.

> ## REVOLUTIONARY REVELATIONS
> James Monroe had been as generous with his money as he was with his time on behalf of the United States. He was reduced in the 1820s to asking the government for reimbursement for his expenses. In 1826, Congress approved a payment to him of $30,000. Magnanimously, it authorized another token amount after his death to purchase his papers from his heirs.

James Monroe may have left this earth financially dependent, but his service to the nation was priceless.

GOUVERNEUR MORRIS

New York, New York
January 31, 1752–November 6, 1816
Hard to Take at Times

Gouverneur Morris, one of the principal writers of the United States Constitution, entered the limelight in the early 1770s. Over the course of his adult years, he fought with his family over the issue of allegiance to independence, served in the army in the Revolutionary War, left the country for ten years, came back, and picked up where he left off. The man with the oddly spelled name was a boon to the United States throughout its growing-up years.

Family Feud

Not many people were gifted enough to enter King's College at age twelve. Gouverneur Morris was one of the few. He began his studies in 1764 and graduated from the college four years later. Too young to start a career at age sixteen, he went on to earn a master's degree in 1771, and followed that with three years of study with the noted New York law scholar William Smith.

Smith, a fervid opponent of British tax policies, introduced Morris to leading New York patriots such as John Jay and Alexander Hamilton. They helped Morris begin his political career.

Once Morris passed the bar exam, he entered the political arena. In 1775, he was elected to the independence-minded, similarly named— and extralegal—New York Provincial Congress, which patriots organized as an alternative to the colony's "official" pro-British legislative body, the Province of New York Assembly. The New York Provincial Congress immediately declared itself the official government on May 22, 1775.

Morris's commitment to independence extracted a dear price: a schism with his family and friends. One of his pet peeves during the Revolutionary War era was Tories, a faction that included his mother, half-brother, and even his mentor William Smith, who became a Tory because he did not favor the New Yorkers' move toward independence.

Early in the war Morris advocated reasoning with colonists who stayed loyal to the king. Later, he supported harsher methods, such as tarring and feathering, whippings, and confiscation of property.

Morris's half-brother, Staats Long Morris (1728–1800), fought in the British army, and became a major general. After the Constitutional Convention of 1787 ended, Gouverneur bought the family estate in New York City from him and moved in.

Morris was unperturbed by the family rift at first. The loss of family ties did not deter him from seeking independence for the colonies.

Politics and War: Whatever It Takes

Morris served in the New York Provincial Congress for two years and the Continental Congress for another two (1777–79).

In 1778, patriots formed a committee to meet with British Prime Minister Lord North's conciliation commissioners. Morris chaired the committee and presented a report adopted by a unanimous vote of Congress that declared that the recognition of independence must precede any negotiations for peace.

He also served in the army for a while, even though he was exempt because of his status as a congressional delegate. And he maintained his separation from his family, although he and his mother later reconciled.

Morris moved to Philadelphia in 1780 and resumed his law career. There he published a series of papers on finance and served as the assistant to superintendent of finance Robert Morris (no relation). He prepared an illuminating report in 1782 that discussed coinage and its inclusion in the American currency system. He suggested that the nation base its currency on the decimal system. But it was not until after the war ended that Gouverneur Morris demonstrated his true value to the United States.

REVOLUTIONARY REVELATIONS

Gouverneur Morris invented the word "cent."

Some Bizarre Ideas

The state of Pennsylvania elected Morris to represent it at the Constitutional Convention of 1787. That was a surprise to Morris. He had a reputation for bluntness and cynicism that he suspected would not be tolerated at the convention. He attended nonetheless—and became one of the lead authors of the U.S. Constitution.

REVOLUTIONARY REVELATIONS

Gouverneur Morris had experience writing constitutions. He had written almost the entire New York Constitution a decade earlier.

Morris had some bizarre ideas about what he wanted for the new U.S. government. He opted for a strong executive who could stay in office as long as he exhibited good behavior and an aristocratic Senate appointed by the president for life. He also tried to insert a clause that guaranteed in perpetuity the political supremacy of the states east of the Allegheny Mountains. Those measures failed.

On the other hand, he helped secure the executive veto and preserve the popular vote for president by defeating a proposal allowing the legislature to elect the president. After the debate over the Constitution ended, Morris wrote the final draft and then went back to New York.

From Pillar to Post

Morris left the United States on a business trip in 1789 and did not return for a decade.

While he was in Europe, he served as the American minister to France. But in a throwback to his reputation as an outspoken cynic back home, he openly showed contempt for the ongoing French Revolution. The French government asked the United States to recall him, which it did. He came home and picked up where he left off, resuming his law career and re-entering politics. He served three years in the United States Senate and took an interest in improving transportation from the eastern part of the country to the interior. He was active in a number of ventures, such as spearheading the project to build the Erie Canal, which contributed significantly to the western development of the United States.

Morris being Morris, he often aggravated other politicians. He was outspoken against the War of 1812 to the point where he promoted the creation of a northern confederacy of states to eliminate the rule of the "Virginia dynasty." It was radical proposals like this that separated Morris from his contemporaries and the views of the Founding Fathers.

As critical as he could be sometimes, Morris never lost his love for a free and independent United States. That is what he had worked so hard for throughout his career. Some people had to have a strong constitution to stomach him at times but because of his efforts, that is what the United States ended up with: a strong constitution.

ROBERT MORRIS

Liverpool, England
January 20, 1734–May 8, 1806
America's Financial Guru

Robert Morris was the Founding Fathers' go-to person when they needed financial advice. He served at various times—and often simultaneously—during the Revolutionary era as the chairman of the Secret Committee of Trade and the Pennsylvania Committee on Safety, a member of the Committee on Correspondence, the superintendent of finance, and agent of marine. Morris was also a U.S. Senator from Pennsylvania; signer of the Declaration of Independence, the Articles of Confederation, and the United States Constitution; a delegate to the Second Continental Congress . . . and that was just a start. Despite his accomplishments, he ended his business career in debtors' prison, which was not the fate either he or the Founding Fathers anticipated. He was the only Founding Father to suffer that fate.

Financing a Revolution

When the Revolutionary War began, Morris was a business partner with Thomas Willing in Philadelphia. At the time, their mercantile venture, which included shipping and real estate operations, among others, was the largest business of its kind in the city. Morris had something that the revolution's leaders needed: financial acumen. He also had the ability to produce the supplies and products the government needed to support the war effort. His politics were unpredictable at best.

Willing to Follow

The delegates to the Second Continental Congress in Philadelphia were not sure which way Morris would vote on independence as they debated the issue. He voted against the resolution of independence on

FEDERAL FACTS

From 1775 to 1777, the federal government awarded nearly $500,000 in contracts to Willing and Morris, and another $290,000 to other partnerships in which Morris was involved. The government's total purchases were $2 million.

July 1, 1776. The next day he did not vote at all. After Congress adopted the resolution on July 4, he signed it. From that point on he threw himself into the American cause, primarily as a financier.

Quotations to Live (and Die) By!

"I AM NOT ONE OF THOSE POLITICIANS THAT RUN TESTY WHEN MY OWN PLANS ARE NOT ADOPTED. I THINK IT IS THE DUTY OF A GOOD CITIZEN TO FOLLOW WHEN HE CANNOT LEAD."

—ROBERT MORRIS, REGARDING THE DECLARATION OF INDEPENDENCE

Washington Turns to Morris

By the end of 1776, the federal government was in dire financial straits. That was particularly stressful for George Washington, who needed the money to supply troops to fight the British. Congress thoughtfully ordered that $5 million worth of paper money be issued to help him. But few people outside the government were willing to use the currency.

Washington, who was not above putting Morris on the spot occasionally, appealed to him to raise enough hard money to back the government-issued currency. Even the normally confident Morris was not sure he could oblige.

Morris had a reputation for honesty and integrity among the people who knew him best. While he was trying to figure out a way to raise the hard currency Washington requested, he met a wealthy Quaker who was aware of the quandary. The gentleman asked Morris what security he provided for a loan. "My note and my honor," Morris said. That was enough for the potential lender. The next day Morris forwarded $50,000 to General Washington.

Even though he doubted his own abilities at times, Morris continued tirelessly throughout the war to raise funds from various sources. He used his personal credit frequently. Morris and several Philadelphians established a bank in the city that sustained the army's operations for most of 1780.

In 1781, when Washington was having trouble raising funds to conduct his campaign to chase the British out of Virginia, Morris borrowed $20,000 from French navy commander Count François-Joseph de Grasse. He promised to repay it in October, although he had no idea where he would get the money. De Grasse provided the loan, which helped Washington drive General Charles Cornwallis and his British forces out of Virginia.

Luckily for Morris, Colonel Henry Laurens arrived in Boston on August 25 that year with $1 million that he had secured from the French government to support the American cause. Morris used part of that subsidy to repay de Grasse.

Morris continued to apply his financial wizardry through the rest of the war—but with a title. Congress named him the superintendent of finance in 1781. Having a title did not make his job any easier. Nevertheless, he continued to find ways to finance the war and get the government on sound footing afterwards, using his own and other people's money, until he stepped down from his post in 1784.

Personal Profit

Morris was not entirely selfless in his efforts; he did profit personally from the war. He had his own fleet of privateers that seized British merchant vessels. Then he helped sell their cargoes when they arrived in port and pocketed part of the revenue. While he was superintendent of finance, he maintained silent partnerships in many of the companies that were doing business with the federal government.

His efforts to enrich himself notwithstanding, Morris worked diligently to earn the label "Financier of the Revolution." Sadly, he was not as successful at financing his own dealings after the war ended.

FEDERAL FACTS

Morris took his responsibilities as superintendent of finance seriously: He cut government spending significantly by using competitive bidding for contracts, tightened accounting procedures, demanded that the states forward to the federal government their full shares of money and supplies, proposed a national bank, and conceived a plan to eliminate the federal government's debt—which the states defeated.

Off to Prison

A series of financial setbacks after the war led to financial ruin for Morris. The Panic of 1797 affected his extensive land holdings adversely. He was imprisoned for debt in February 1798 and remained incarcerated until August 1801.

The man who almost single-handedly kept the country afloat financially in its fledgling years died five years after he left prison. He was in poor health and practically penniless. But he still had his pride, a supportive wife of thirty-seven years, and a legacy as a founder of a country that had relied on him for its existence.

JEREMIAH O'BRIEN

Kittery, Maine
1744–October 5, 1818
A Man Without a Plan

Machias, Maine (at the time, Maine was part of Massachusetts) businessman Jeremiah O'Brien earned the title of "Father of the Navy" as the result of his attack on a British navy warship in June 1775. He was thrust into his role by default. Unlike the Founding Fathers, O'Brien did not have time to think about how to break away from Britain. Acting without congressional guidance or much of a plan, he set off the naval part of the Revolutionary War and left the Founding Fathers to pick up the pieces.

No Lumber for Boston

Jeremiah and his brothers Gideon, John, William, Dennis, and Joseph were ardent patriots and business owners in Massachusetts. They and their father, Morris, were in the lumber business in Machias.

The citizens of Machias were in dire need of supplies from Boston in the spring of 1775. Because of British naval activities along the New England coast, supplies were hard to come by via sea, which was the most expedient transportation route at the time. Conversely, it was difficult for local lumber producers to send their products to Boston.

That was the situation when Boston merchant Captain Ichabod Jones arrived in Machias on June 9, 1775, with two sloops, *Unity* and *Polly*, carrying badly needed provisions. A British navy schooner, *Margaretta*, commanded by James Moore, accompanied Jones's ships to protect them.

Jones enraged the citizens of Machias by demanding that they sign a paper agreeing to trade their lumber to the British for the supplies he brought with him, and also guaranteeing to protect him and his property. Jones refused to distribute supplies to those who would not sign.

Then, Jones asked Moore to bring *Margaretta* close to the docks with guns ready to fire, presumably in an attempt to intimidate the citizens into agreeing to Jones's terms. The intimidation attempt failed.

The patriots in Machias hatched a plot to capture Moore and his officers while they attended a church service, intending to prevent them from accompanying Jones back to Boston. The British caught wind of the plot, jumped out the windows of the church, boarded their ship, and escaped to the safety of the harbor. That was when the O'Briens and their friends entered the fray.

The O'Briens acted spontaneously, which was often the case among patriots at the beginning of the Revolutionary War.

The O'Briens Show "Unity"

The O'Briens secretly invited their friends from nearby Mispecka and Pleasant River to join them in their private revolution. Once the *Margaretta* reached the safety of the bay, O'Brien, his brothers, Joseph Wheaton, and several other patriots—about forty men in all—sprang into action. Armed with guns and the only three rounds of ammunition they had among them, swords, axes, pitchforks, and anything else they could get their hands on, the men jumped aboard the *Unity* and sailed toward the *Margaretta*. Another group, led by Captain Benjamin Foster, joined O'Brien in a smaller sloop.

The battle was short and swift. O'Brien led a masterful attack on the *Margaretta* in that June 12 encounter. Captain Moore, realizing that he was outmanned and outmaneuvered, tried to escape. He failed—and paid with his life. In one hour the patriots killed Captain Moore, his helmsman, and two other crew members. They wounded five more. One American was killed during the battle; six were wounded, one of whom died later. (Conflicting reports suggest that there were ten British sailors and marines killed and ten wounded, compared to four Americans killed and nine wounded.)

O'Brien became an instant—and emboldened—hero. The battle that earned Machias the title of the "Lexington of the Sea" was the launch point for additional exploits by Captain O'Brien.

FEDERAL FACTS

According to the June 14, 1775, official report of the Machias Committee of Correspondence to the Massachusetts Provincial Congress, O'Brien's little navy captured "four double fortified three pounders and fourteen swivels and a number of small arms, which we took with the tender, besides a very small quantity of ammunition, etc."

O'Brien Goes to Washington

Following his victory at Machias, O'Brien refitted *Unity* with *Margaretta's* guns, renamed it *Machias Liberty*, and sailed off aboard his privateer to find more prizes. He and his crew captured two armed enemy schooners and their crews off the Bay of Fundy in Canada and took them to Cambridge. The ships O'Brien captured—the *Diligence*, a British coast-survey vessel, and her tender—had been dispatched from Halifax to retake *Margaretta*.

He delivered the prisoners directly to General Washington. The general was impressed. He recommended to Massachusetts government officials that they appoint O'Brien to command of his prizes. They agreed, and awarded O'Brien the first captain's commission in the Massachusetts State Navy.

O'Brien's navy career was short, but adventurous. He maintained his command of *Machias Liberty* for two years. His brother William served as a lieutenant. Another brother, John, was a lieutenant aboard the captured *Diligence*.

FEDERAL FACTS

Even though the Continental Navy did not exist at this stage of the war, historians consider the naval battle at Machias to be the first time British colors were struck to those of the United States.

The provincial government assigned *Machias Liberty* and *Diligence* to intercept supplies for the British troops. They operated along the northeastern coast for a year and a half, taking several prizes. After that, Jeremiah took command of a privateer named *Hannibal* that his brother John and others had built at Newburyport, Massachusetts.

Two British frigates captured *Hannibal* off the New York coast in the late 1770s. The British confined O'Brien for six months on a guard ship, *Jersey*, then sent him to England and held him in the infamous Mill Prison. He escaped after a few months and made his way back to Maine.

Later, he received an appointment as the federal collector for the Port of Machias, which he held until his death. The navy he fathered lives on.

JAMES OTIS JR.

West Barnstable, Massachusetts
February 5, 1725–May 23, 1783
Hidden Father of a Nation

James Otis Jr., one of the more tragic figures of the revolutionary era, was among America's most influential patriot leaders in the 1760s. But, in one of those freak events that alter history, his career was cut short by an irate Bostonian wielding a cane in a fit of bad temper. Had Otis not suffered bouts of insanity for fourteen years before he died, he, not Thomas Jefferson, might be hailed as the principal author of the Declaration of Independence.

Becoming a Patriot

James Otis Jr. was not anti-Britain early in his career, but he became that way. He graduated from Harvard in 1743, when he was eighteen. There he studied law under noted jurist Jeremiah Gridley. Five years later, he was admitted to the bar. Eventually, he became a public employee, but not for long.

In 1756, Otis accepted a position as the king's advocate general to the vice-admiralty court of Boston. He did not like what he saw in his responsibilities as advocate general, part of which involved prosecuting smugglers.

The British were heavy-handed in their law enforcement policies regarding smuggling. They had passed a series of Acts of Trade and

Navigation between 1650 and 1767 that subordinated the colonists' interests to their own. Those laws aggravated the Americans.

When the British passed a tax-laden Molasses Act in 1733 to protect British West Indies planters from competition provided by their non-British producers in the French West Indies, it infuriated the colonists—especially the distillers who needed the commodities to make their own spirits.

Very few people in America took paying the tax seriously. That rankled the British and led to more austere taxes in 1764, when they replaced the Molasses Act with the Sugar Act. The colonists did not like the new tax any more than the one it replaced. That was one of the reasons they decided to split from the British.

FEDERAL FACTS

The Molasses Act made the products from the British West Indies more expensive for American distillers and inhibited them from importing such goods. In what was to become a time-honored tradition among the Americans, they ignored the act, along with the Acts of Trade and Navigation. They figured it was more profitable to smuggle in rum and spirits, molasses, and sugar than pay the taxes on them.

 Quotations to Live (and Die) By!

"IF WE ARE NOT REPRESENTED, WE ARE SLAVES."
—JAMES OTIS JR., REGARDING THE SUGAR ACT OF 1764

The Teacher Teaches the Student a Lesson

Otis felt guilty about prosecuting smugglers, because the innovative British had introduced a new legal tactic called writs of assistance to help them find, try, and convict the violators. The writs did not assist anybody but the British.

The writs of assistance were general search warrants that allowed customs officials to enter houses and places of business whenever and wherever they pleased to look for unspecified contraband. Otis believed the writs of assistance were unconstitutional, even if the colonists did not have a written constitution. He did something about it.

Otis resigned his position in 1761 to defend smugglers against the vagaries of the writs of assistance.

He presented a spirited defense against the writs of assistance in a classic February 1761 court case. Otis's eloquent five-hour presentation to the court explaining why the writs were unconstitutional captured the attention of a young attorney sitting in the courtroom, John Adams.

 Quotations to Live (and Die) By!

"A MAN'S HOUSE IS HIS CASTLE; AND WHILST HE IS QUIET, HE IS AS WELL GUARDED AS A PRINCE IN HIS CASTLE. THIS WRIT, IF IT SHOULD BE DECLARED LEGAL, WOULD TOTALLY ANNIHILATE THIS PRIVILEGE. CUSTOM-HOUSE OFFICERS MAY ENTER OUR HOUSES WHEN THEY PLEASE; WE ARE COMMANDED TO PERMIT THEIR ENTRY. THEIR MENIAL SERVANTS MAY ENTER, MAY BREAK LOCKS, BARS, AND EVERYTHING IN THEIR WAY; AND WHETHER THEY BREAK THROUGH MALICE OR REVENGE, NO MAN, NO COURT MAY INQUIRE."

—JAMES OTIS

Despite Otis's brilliant performance, the court upheld the writs of assistance. That disappointed Otis and his clients, but it did not dissuade him from continuing his resistance to the writs or the laws with which they were associated. Like other patriots (including his sister, Mercy Otis Warren), he turned to the pen as his weapon of choice.

The Pamphlet Is Mightier Than the Sword

In 1764, Otis produced an insightful pamphlet, *Rights of the British Colonies Asserted and Proved.* He also wrote *A Vindication of the British Colonies* and *Considerations on Behalf of the Colonies*, in which he attacked the British idea of "virtual representation" in Parliament (the idea that one can be represented by a decision-making process without being able to vote for those who make the decisions) and the philosophy of the Navigation Acts, which he claimed inhibited the trade of the colonists' manufactured products.

Otis was not afraid to challenge the British in court or writing, join organizations formed to help the colonists express their distaste for the king's policies, or take action against them. He became a member of the Sons of Liberty, and attended the Stamp Act Congress of 1765. Significantly, he introduced the motion in the Massachusetts assembly proposing that the congress be convened.

 Quotations to Live (and Die) By!

"AN ACT AGAINST THE CONSTITUTION IS VOID; AN ACT AGAINST NATURAL EQUITY IS VOID. TAXATION WITHOUT REPRESENTATION IS TYRANNY."
—JAMES OTIS, REGARDING THE STAMP ACT OF 1765

Taking a Beating

In September 1769, Otis wrote a satire of the local commissioners of customs that appeared in the *Boston Gazette*. John Robinson, an enraged Boston customhouse official, reacted to what he perceived as a libelous account of him and confronted Otis the next day, attacking him with a cane. Robinson beat Otis viciously around the head with his weapon. The aftereffects of the attack produced periods of mental instability in

Otis that plagued him throughout the rest of his life and rendered him incapable of participating in public affairs at a time when his guidance was needed.

Otis achieved a moral victory as a result of the affair. He sued Robinson and was awarded £2,000 in damages. But Robinson offered a public apology, which Otis accepted and declared that he was satisfied. That ended the affair—but Otis paid the price in the long run.

Sadly, instead of becoming a patriot leader, Otis became a figure of public ridicule. He spent his days wandering around Boston, subjected to jeers from people who forgot or ignored his significant contributions on their behalf prior to 1769. History has not been kind to James Otis Jr. He does not receive the amount of credit due him for his contributions to the patriots' cause. Strangely enough, he did not have a lot of time to consider them after the Revolutionary War ended.

Misfortune plagued him once again on May 23, 1783, when a bolt of lightning struck and killed him. That was a bizarre ending for the once-popular patriot whose strokes of genius had helped pave the way for American independence.

⚍ THOMAS PAINE ⚍

Thetford, England
January 29, 1737–June 8, 1809
Roving Revolutionary

Thomas Paine is sometimes called "The Father of the Revolution," though the seeds of the revolution were planted long before he arrived in the United States. Paine came from England to Philadelphia and earned national prominence in 1776 when he published *Common Sense*, in which he ardently supported American independence. He also served in the army for a short time during the Revolutionary War. His biggest contribution was *The Crisis*, a pamphlet that encouraged Americans to remain resolved.

Fired with Enthusiasm: Fired from Everything Else

Young Thomas Paine exasperated his father and everyone around him. He flunked out of school before he was twelve. He served an apprenticeship with his father as a corsetmaker but refused to be tied down, so he tried his hand as a sailor. That did not work either.

Losing jobs, businesses, and the people he loved was commonplace for Paine in his younger years. He started a business as a corsetmaker in Sandwich, Kent, in 1759, the same year he married Mary Lambert. His business failed. They moved to Margate, England, to get a fresh start. Mary became pregnant, but went into early labor. Lamentably, she and the child died in 1760—less than a year after their wedding.

REVOLUTIONARY REVELATIONS

Thomas Paine also worked as a servant and schoolteacher. According to some accounts, he was an ordained Church of England clergyman—even though he had been raised as a Quaker.

Later, he obtained a job in 1768 as a tax officer in Lewes, England, working for a government for which he had no particular fondness. Paine functioned as a tax officer for four years. During that time he was fired twice. After being fired the first time, he opened a tobacco shop and married his landlord's daughter, Elizabeth Olive, on March 26, 1771. The shop and the marriage failed. He was able to obtain a second appointment as a tax officer.

Although Paine was unable to hold a job, he found his true calling during his time with the tax authority. He wrote his first political tract in 1772, a twenty-one page pamphlet called *The Case of the Officers of Excise*. In it, he argued on behalf of his fellow tax officers in Lewes for a pay raise and better working conditions. Two years later he was discharged for being absent from his post without permission.

 Quotations to Live (and Die) By!

"SOCIETY IS PRODUCED BY OUR WANTS AND GOVERNMENT BY OUR WICKEDNESS."

—THOMAS PAINE

REVOLUTIONARY REVELATIONS

Paine had 4,000 copies of *The Case of the Officers of Excise* printed. Among the first recipients were the members of Parliament. They were not amused.

He moved to London, where he met Benjamin Franklin in the early 1770s. Franklin was impressed by Paine's passion. The elder statesman suggested to Paine that a man of his talents—which had not yet been developed fully—should move to America. Paine followed Franklin's advice.

The Power of the Press

Paine arrived in Philadelphia on November 30, 1774. He began writing articles for *Pennsylvania Magazine* to gain journalistic experience. During his first year in the city he developed an appreciation for the American's pursuit of independence.

On January 10, 1776, Paine published his short work, *Common Sense*, in which he attacked the British form of government and its constitution, opposed reconciliation with Britain, called for an American declaration of independence, and espoused a republican style of government in the new country. The controversial pamphlet was an immediate success.

Paine became an instant hero in America. His words were a clarion call to independence—and war. Paine put down his pen and joined the army. He picked it up again quickly.

Quotations to Live (and Die) By!

"I FIND *COMMON SENSE* IS WORKING A POWERFUL CHANGE IN THE MINDS OF MEN."
—GEORGE WASHINGTON

Never Lose a Good Crisis

Even as Paine joined the army in its retreat across New Jersey, he continued writing. He authored a series of pamphlets known collectively as *The*

American Crisis, which bolstered soldiers' flagging morale and kept the spirit of independence alive.

Quotations to Live (and Die) By!

"THESE ARE THE TIMES THAT TRY MEN'S SOULS."
—THOMAS PAINE

Paine kept writing as the war drew to a close, and Americans continued to draw inspiration from his words. Finally, in *The Crisis, XIII*, he wrote, "The times that tried men's souls are over—and the greatest and completest revolution the world ever knew, gloriously and happily accomplished." Then he disappeared.

After the fighting ended, there was no need for Paine's pen. He busied himself with more worldly issues, like wheedling money out of Congress. Since he was in dire financial straits after the war, he petitioned various governments for compensation. Congress eventually awarded him $3,000, and New York gave him a farm in New Rochelle it had seized from a Tory sympathizer.

REVOLUTIONARY REVELATIONS

Thomas Paine tried to earn some money on his own after the Revolutionary War by developing a smokeless candle and an iron bridge. Like most of his prior business ventures, his inventions did not pan out.

Finally, disenchanted with the United States and its lack of support for him, he moved back to Europe, bouncing between France and England. He wrote pamphlets in support of the French revolutionaries, for which he went to jail.

Paine languished in Luxembourg Prison from December 28, 1793, to November 4, 1794. The new U.S. ambassador to France, James Monroe, finally secured his release.

A Sad End

Friends were getting hard to come by for Paine as the nineteenth century began. He had begun a series of attacks on religion, which was making him persona non grata in Europe. Thomas Jefferson came to his rescue and invited him back to the United States.

News of Paine's attacks on religion reached the United States long before he did in October 1802. When he got back to what he thought was friendly territory, former friends greeted him with less than open arms.

Paine spent his final years in New York City, suffering from alcoholism, poverty, and poor health. He had become a subject of derision, rather than a returning hero. He died at the age of seventy-two, and was buried at his farm in New Rochelle.

 Quotations to Live (and Die) By!

"He had lived long, did some good and much harm."
—Thomas Paine's obituary, *New York Citizen* newspaper

Only five people attended Paine's funeral. That was a sad farewell for the man many people called "The Father of the Revolution."

CHARLES COTESWORTH PINCKNEY

Charleston, South Carolina
February 25, 1746–August 16, 1825

Pinckney was a legislator, a soldier, an envoy to France, an unsuccessful candidate for U.S. president (twice)—and proud to serve in whatever capacity he could. He was a nationalist who had a vision of the United States as a country with a central government, not just a confederation of states, which distinguished him from most of his contemporaries who had not thought that far ahead.

Homecoming

By any measure, Charles Cotesworth Pinckney, not to be confused with his first cousin once removed and fellow prominent South Carolina politician Charles Pinckney, should have been a Tory. His father, South Carolina's agent in Britain, moved the family to England in 1753. Charles was educated at Oxford University and studied law at Middle Temple. He lived in the "Mother Country" for sixteen years. British affiliations notwithstanding, Charles threw in his lot with the colonies in their spat with Britain when he returned to South Carolina in 1769 with his law degree in hand, ready to start his own practice and enter politics.

His first foray into politics occurred in 1769, when he was elected to the South Carolina legislature. Four years later, he was appointed to a position as a regional attorney general. He had to put his career on hold to serve his country as an officer in the Continental Army.

REVOLUTIONARY REVELATIONS

Unlike many of the patriots who helped build the American Revolution, Charles C. Pinckney did not participate in the Continental Congresses.

As did so many men in the mid-1700s, Pinckney joined the militia. He did not enlist because he wanted to march off to war. It was more of a social steppingstone for young men of the genteel persuasion. Pinckney joined the prestigious 1st Regiment of South Carolina militia; his peers elected him as a lieutenant. The training came in handy.

Pinckney on Patrol

There was one major difference between Pinckney's view of the embryonic United States and that of his peers. He believed that patriots had to look at the big picture; they had to fight for a united country rather than strictly for their individual states. Consequently, he joined the Continental Army rather than wait for the British to attack South Carolina. As it turned out, he did plenty of fighting in his home state.

REVOLUTIONARY REVELATIONS

Pinckney served dual roles during the Revolutionary War. He was a member of both the lower house of the state legislature and the South Carolina Senate.

Early in the war Pinckney served as an aide-de-camp to General Washington at the battles of Brandywine and Germantown in 1777. He then returned to South Carolina and resumed his duties as a legislator. They were far different from those he had carried out as a soldier.

Leaders in the field started beseeching Pinckney for financial relief and support.

Quotations to Live (and Die) By!

"BE GENEROUS TO YOUR MILITIA. ALLOW THEM EVERY-THING NECESSARY TO TAKE THE FIELD. IT IS NOW TIME TO OPEN YOUR PURSE STRINGS. OUR COUNTRY IS IN DAN-GER. BE MORE BOUNTIFUL THAN YOU HAVE BEEN HITH-ERTO IN THIS PRESENT ADMINISTRATION."

—WILLIAM MOULTRIE IN A JANUARY 10, 1779, LETTER TO CHARLES PINCKNEY

Soon Pinckney was back in the field himself. He served during the siege of Savannah, Georgia, in September and October 1779 and then at Charleston, South Carolina, in 1780. The British captured the entire Continental Army fighting at Charleston, and detained Pinckney as a prisoner of war until 1781. That ended his military involvement in the war.

Idea Man

Pinckney served in the South Carolina legislature from 1786–89, with a brief break to attend the Constitutional Convention in Philadelphia. He offered many ideas as discussions progressed. Many of them were not adopted because they were considered radical. Among them, Pinckney wanted to abolish slavery and allow an unlimited number of soldiers in a standing army. Radical ideas aside, he led the successful ratification effort back home in South Carolina. Mostly, he advocated for a strong federal government.

Quotations to Live (and Die) By!

"THE GREAT ART OF GOVERNMENT IS NOT TO GOVERN TOO MUCH."

—CHARLES COTESWORTH PINCKNEY

REVOLUTIONARY REVELATIONS

At the Constitutional Convention of 1787, Charles Pinckney suggested that U.S. senators serve without pay. He thought they should all be independently wealthy men.

Once the Constitution was adopted, Pinckney became increasingly active in national politics. He turned down offers to serve as the secretary of war and secretary of state, but left the door open for other positions. More importantly, Pinckney and John Adams became good friends—and ran on the same presidential ticket.

Before that happened, President Washington appointed Pinckney in 1796 as minister to France. It was his first trek to Europe in a quarter century, and a most memorable experience—until political reality struck. The French government refused to receive Pinckney, who moved to the Netherlands after his credentials were rejected. His presence in Europe provided a unique opportunity for John Adams, who had replaced Washington as U.S. president. Adams asked Pinckney to join John Marshall and Elbridge Gerry on a committee in Paris to improve diplomatic relations with France, which resulted in the scandalous XYZ affair in 1798.

Running Away from Landslides

French officials offered the Americans a deal regarding the ongoing differences between the two countries in the late 1790s. All the Americans had to do was offer a gift—preferably cash—to three unnamed French people (X, Y, and Z) to settle their differences. If they did, the French might sign a peace treaty.

The so-called XYZ affair ended when the Americans refused to offer the bribe, and the French bid the American envoys a less-than-pleasant adieu.

When Adams ran for reelection as president in 1800, Pinckney was the candidate for vice president. Thomas Jefferson and Aaron Burr defeated them. The election results did not faze Pinckney. They whetted his appetite for future presidential campaigns.

Pinckney tried to win the presidency in 1804 and 1808, first against Thomas Jefferson and then against James Madison. He lost by landslides both times.

As suddenly as Pinckney's national political ambitions surfaced, they disappeared. After his second drubbing in a presidential race, Pinckney returned to the solitude of South Carolina. He involved himself in local and state educational and religious matters.

Charles C. Pinckney is remembered for his fierce loyalty to the United States. That was how he lived his life—and that is how he will be remembered in death.

CAESAR RODNEY

Dover, Delaware
October 7, 1728–June 26, 1784
The Nation's Health above My Own

The lack of a formal education never stopped Caesar Rodney from serving his colony and his country. In a ten-year span, the positions he held in Delaware included high sheriff of Kent County; registrar of wills; recorder of deeds; clerk of the orphan's court; justice of the peace; Colonial assemblyman; Stamp Act Congress delegate; and member of the colony's Committee of Correspondence. Then he got busy. He was elected to the Continental Congress for three terms (1774–76) and served as a major general in the Delaware militia. Rodney cast the deciding vote in 1776 that placed Delaware in the "for independence" column—and he may have done all that simply to push a lost love for a woman out of his mind.

Delaware's Savior

Caesar Rodney came from an undistinguished family but rose to prominence in Delaware politics through hard work and devotion to a cause. His father, a farmer, died when Caesar was seventeen. Nicholas Ridgely, a clerk of the peace in Kent County, became Caesar's guardian and instilled in the young man a love of politics. After that, not even a cancerous growth that covered a large portion of his face could stop him from fighting for freedom from British rule.

Rodney demonstrated his opposition to British tax legislation and willingness to travel to speak out against it as early as 1765, when he attended the Stamp Act Congress in New York City. That was the same year he joined the Committee of Correspondence, whose job it was to coordinate actions against the British with similar committees in other colonies.

Quotations to Live (and Die) By!

"NO ONE WAS EITHER TORY OR WHIG; IT WAS EITHER DEPENDENCE OR INDEPENDENCE."
—CAESAR RODNEY

The Stamp Act Congress, October 7–25, 1765, was the first gathering of delegates from different colonies to protest the new British taxation laws. It was a precursor of the Continental Congress.

It was no surprise that Rodney was elected to represent Delaware at the First Continental Congress in 1774.

Rodney soon proved to the other delegates that he could be depended on when needed to further the cause of independence.

Rodney returned to the Congress in 1775 and 1776. When the question of independence arose, he delivered Delaware, although it took a lot of time and effort for him to cast the crucial vote.

Neither Rain nor Thunder . . .

As the Second Continental Congress debated whether it should vote for independence in 1776, Rodney was back in Sussex County, Delaware, in his capacity as a militia leader. He was investigating rumors about a possible Tory riot, unaware of the drama that was unfolding in Philadelphia. The last thing he wanted was to travel north to cast a vote.

Caesar Rodney was in poor health in 1776, which was normal for him. Frequent asthma attacks and a spreading cancerous growth on his face that he referred to as "that horrid and most obstinate disorder" were sapping his energy, and he needed some rest to combat the effects of both. But when duty called, Rodney responded. He put his country's health above his own, which was typical of him.

REVOLUTIONARY REVELATIONS

Historians speculate that one reason Rodney stayed busy all the time was a sense of loss. He remained a bachelor throughout his life because the woman he loved, Molly Vining, married a rector and died shortly thereafter. Rodney never recovered from his grief over the death of another man's wife.

The Delaware contingent at the Second Continental Congress was in disarray. Thomas McKean was in favor of independence; George Read was not. The Congress did not need Delaware's vote for independence, but it preferred a unanimous vote to impress British authorities with their solidarity. McKean sent a note back to Delaware advising Rodney of the stalemate. Rodney hopped on the nearest horse and sped off to Philadelphia on a harrowing ride.

Quotations to Live (and Die) By!

"I ARRIVED IN CONGRESS (THO DETAINED BY THUNDER AND RAIN) TIME ENOUGH TO GIVE MY VOTE IN THE MATTER OF INDEPENDENCE."

—CAESAR RODNEY IN A JULY 4, 1776, LETTER TO HIS BROTHER, THOMAS RODNEY

Caesar Rodney's dash to Philadelphia made Paul Revere's famous ride look like a lap around a riding ring. He rode eighty miles overnight between Dover and Philadelphia to ensure that his colony voted yes for independence.

After a few twists and turns, the final vote was 13–0 for independence. Rodney helped save the day—and the country.

Rodney's work was done at the Congress. He returned to Delaware to prepare for his participation in the war.

The End Is Near

Delaware played a critical role in the Revolutionary War. The state had a record of always meeting its obligations in supplying troops and materiel. Helping raise those troops and amassing supplies was all that Rodney could do as the fighting continued, with one exception.

On December 26, 1776, General Washington assigned Brigadier General Rodney to command the post at Trenton. His orders were to defend the river crossing at Trenton and send new troops to General Washington. He accomplished both goals, much to Washington's delight.

As the war drew to a close, so did Rodney's political career. Though elected to the national Congress in 1782, he declined because of his poor health. He continued with his responsibilities as Speaker to the Upper House of the Delaware Assembly, but that took a toll on his welfare, too.

REVOLUTIONARY REVELATIONS

No one knows for sure on what date Rodney died or where he was buried. Records show that he was interred on his farm in an unmarked grave on June 28, 1784, where his remains lay for over a century. His body—or possibly a relative's—was exhumed and moved to Christ Church in Wilmington in 1889.

Finally, Rodney's lack of attention to his own health caught up with him. He died on or about June 26, 1784.

There was a certain amount of mystery regarding the circumstances of Caesar Rodney's death and burial. There was none, however, about his life. He made sure Delaware voted for independence, for which he will never be forgotten.

BENJAMIN RUSH

Byberry, Pennsylvania
December 24, 1745–April 19, 1813
Bleeding Heart

Benjamin Rush was one of the most flexible patriots in the Revolutionary War era. He saved lives as a doctor and helped save a country as a politician. Rush earned a medical degree from the University of Edinburgh in Scotland, served in the American medical corps during the Revolutionary War and as the treasurer of the U.S. Mint, signed the Declaration of Independence, and taught at the University of Pennsylvania. Significantly, he was the intermediary who coordinated the reconciliation between John Adams and Thomas Jefferson. Almost everybody liked and respected Rush. Almost.

School Days

When Benjamin Rush's father, John, died, Benjamin's mother sent the five-year-old to live with his uncle, Samuel Finley, who ran a private school, West Nottingham Academy, in Maryland. Finley convinced Benjamin to become a doctor.

Rush began his medical studies in Philadelphia, and completed them at the University of Edinburgh. After a brief stay in Europe, he returned to America in 1769 and threw himself into the political struggle for independence.

Rush joined the Sons of Liberty in Philadelphia, began writing political essays advocating independence, and served in the Pennsylvania Provincial Conference. That led to his appointment as a member of the Second Continental Congress in 1776 and his signature on the Declaration of Independence.

 Quotations to Live (and Die) By!

"LIBERTY WITHOUT VIRTUE WOULD BE NO BLESSING TO US."
—BENJAMIN RUSH

One of his major achievements was encouraging Thomas Paine to publish *Common Sense*, which Rush titled. Ever mindful of his reputation in Philadelphia, Rush was relieved that someone other than himself was willing to write such an anti-British political tract.

Rush to Judgment

In 1777, Rush became surgeon general of the middle department of the Continental Army. His penchant for contentiousness on some subjects came to the fore in that capacity. He and Dr. William Shippen Jr., the director general of hospitals for the army, clashed in their views of how the medical service should be run.

Quotations to Live (and Die) By!

"I SUGGESTED TO [MR. PAINE] THAT HE HAD NOTHING TO FEAR FROM THE POPULAR ODIUM TO WHICH SUCH A PUBLICATION MIGHT EXPOSE HIM, FOR HE COULD LIVE ANYWHERE, BUT THAT MY PROFESSION AND CONNEC- TIONS, WHICH TIED ME TO PHILADELPHIA . . . FORBADE ME TO COME FORWARD AS A PIONEER IN THAT IMPOR- TANT CONTROVERSY."

—BENJAMIN RUSH

Rush blamed Dr. Shippen for the miserable health conditions plaguing the Continental Army. He filed a formal complaint against Shippen, which Congress investigated and rejected.

Rush's biggest gaffe was siding with a group of people who tried to oust General Washington as commander in chief. In 1778, Rush sent an anonymous letter to Patrick Henry campaigning for Washington's removal—forgetting that his distinctive handwriting would easily identify the letter writer as Benjamin Rush. Once the details of his letter emerged, he had one choice. Rush resigned from the army.

Quotations to Live (and Die) By!

"CONTROVERSY IS ONLY DREADED BY THE ADVOCATES OF ERROR."

—BENJAMIN RUSH

Rush Hour

Undaunted, Rush resumed his civilian life—as busy as ever. New opportunities abounded for him. He was appointed to the staff of Pennsylvania Hospital in 1783, then elected to the Pennsylvania convention to ratify the new U.S. Constitution, which it did on December 12, 1787. He became professor of medical theory and clinical practice at the University of Pennsylvania in 1791.

REVOLUTIONARY REVELATIONS

Even though he was respected as a doctor, Rush relied on practically the same remedy for every disease: bleeding, the withdrawal of varying quantities of blood from a patient to treat illness and disease. His obstinate nature revealed itself in this respect. The treatment method faded into medical history toward the end of the eighteenth century, but Rush continued to apply it.

He also wrote numerous works on a variety of topics, ranging from *An Account of the Bilious Remitting Yellow Fever* to *Considerations on the Injustice and Impolicy of Punishing Murder by Death* and *Essays, Literary, Moral & Philosophical*.

Among his other accomplishments, Rush established Dickinson College in Carlisle, Pennsylvania, and the Philadelphia Society for Alleviating the Miseries of Public Prisons. His hands seemed to be into everything going on in Philadelphia at the end of the eighteenth century.

REVOLUTIONARY REVELATIONS

The Royal Swedish Academy of Sciences inducted Rush as a member in 1794 in recognition of his contributions to medicine and the sciences.

Rush dropped out of politics as the nineteenth century began. He contented himself with crusading against a variety of causes, among them slavery, alcohol, classical education, and tobacco.

Perhaps Rush's most significant accomplishment as a doctor occurred in 1793, when Philadelphia was ravaged by an outbreak of yellow fever. At one point, there were only three doctors available to treat the 6,000 people affected by the fever. He worked long hours to stem the epidemic. Rush succeeded in doing so by administering a new and improved treatment of calomel and jalap combined. His remedy helped to curb the outbreak.

Amazingly, the yellow fever outbreak did not affect Rush. He worked tirelessly for another twenty years trying to cure other ills, medicinal and social alike. Finally, an unspecified illness led to his death in 1813.

REVOLUTIONARY REVELATIONS

One of Rush's final acts was to express his regrets in a roundabout way for attacking George Washington. He told John Adams in an 1812 letter, "[Washington] was the highly favored instrument whose patriotism and name contributed greatly to the establishment of the independence of the United States."

HAYM SALOMON

Lissa, Poland
April 7, 1740 – January 6, 1785
Dear Haym: Army's Broke, Send Money-G.W.

When the perpetually broke George Washington and Congress needed money, they generally contacted Haym Salomon, a financier and occasional spy who could always be counted on to raise funds— often from his own pockets. The U.S. government owed Salomon a big debt after the war ended, but it never paid him a penny—thus he died penniless.

A Well-Spoken Gentleman

Prior to immigrating to the United States, Haym Salomon gadded around Europe learning about finances and picking up languages. By the time he reached America in 1772, he spoke eight different languages fluently and knew enough about finance and business to open his own business and become a dealer in foreign securities.

He wasn't above bribing a British prison guard on occasion or possibly engaging in arson, which a true Founding Father would not do. Then again, Salomon was not a diplomat. He was a financier who was good at what he did. George Washington never asked Salomon where he got the money. He was just happy to get it.

One of the people who befriended Salomon was Alexander McDougall, a member of the Sons of Liberty. Salomon became an active member of the organization, which eventually landed him in jail—and almost in a noose.

A mysterious fire destroyed much of New York City in 1776. The fire began on September 20, 1776. The flames burned 493 houses—almost one quarter of the city. The British army had planned to house its troops in those houses.

Quotations to Live (and Die) By!

"PROVIDENCE, OR SOME GOOD HONEST FELLOW, HAS DONE MORE FOR US THAN WE WERE DISPOSED TO DO FOR OURSELVES."

—GEORGE WASHINGTON, AFTER THE NEW YORK FIRE

Salomon was among the Sons arrested for allegedly setting the fire. He subtly let the British know that he spoke German fluently. They offered to upgrade his living conditions and improve the quality of his food if he would act as an interpreter for the Hessians (German soldiers contracted by King George III to supplement his regular army). He was happy to oblige.

Salomon was an opportunist. He seized the chance to be an interpreter to serve the patriots' cause.

Since the British did not speak German, and the Hessians did not speak English, Salomon "interpreted." What he was really doing was trying to encourage the Hessians to desert—and approximately 500 of them did! But the British paroled him before they all disappeared, or before they caught on to what he was doing.

Well, I'll Be Hanged

The British arrested Salomon again in 1778, this time for spying. They confiscated his property and sentenced him to hang, but he bribed a guard who helped him escape. He fled to Philadelphia, where his wife, Rachel, and their child joined him.

Salomon was penniless, but that had never stopped him before. He opened a brokerage business and accepted an offer from the French minister as paymaster general of the French forces fighting alongside the Americans.

REVOLUTIONARY REVELATIONS

Salomon's ability to speak numerous languages paid off again in Philadelphia. While he was there, the Dutch and Spanish governments hired him to sell the securities that financed loans they had made to the Continental Congress.

Quotations to Live (and Die) By!

"I AM A JEW; IT IS MY OWN NATION; I DO NOT DESPAIR THAT WE SHALL OBTAIN EVERY OTHER PRIVILEGE THAT WE ASPIRE TO ENJOY ALONG WITH OUR FELLOW-CITIZENS."

—HAYM SALOMON

Salomon led an active life in Philadelphia. He was a member of the governing council of the city's Congregation Mikveh Israel and served as the treasurer of its society for indigent travelers. He also took part in the country's first rabbinic court of arbitration. More importantly, he led the successful fight to repeal the test oath that prohibited Jews and other non-Christians from holding public office in Pennsylvania.

Paying Debts and Losing Money

The nation was on the brink of financial ruin in 1781. Then Congress established the office of finance and appointed Robert Morris to run it. Morris and Salomon worked together to save the United States from fiscal ruin. Salomon became an effective broker of bills of exchange to help the federal government pay its expenses. And, he loaned his personal funds to several members of the government.

Salomon was not completely altruistic. He charged the people to whom he loaned money interest and commissions. He loaned money to folks ranging from Thomas Jefferson to General Friedrich Wilhelm August Heinrich Ferdinand von Steuben, the Prussian-born inspector general and major general of the Continental Army. In the long run, it did not matter what rates Salomon charged. Nobody paid him back.

FEDERAL FACTS

Congress did not have the authority to tax anyone directly during the war, although it could levy taxes on imported goods. It relied mostly on requests to the individual states to raise money. Most of the time the states ignored the pleas. The federal government's only recourse was to borrow money from friendly foreign governments, such as the French and Dutch.

 Quotations to Live (and Die) By!

"I HAVE FOR SOME TIME . . . BEEN A PENSIONER ON THE FAVOR OF HAYM SALOMON, A JEW BROKER."
—JAMES MADISON

One Last Miracle

As the war drew to a close, Washington had a chance to chase the British out of Virginia. All he needed was $20,000 to finance his campaign. He might as well have asked for an army of aliens to arrive in spaceships to provide artillery. Robert Morris told Washington he had no money and no credit. The general gave him one order: Send for Haym Salomon. Morris did. Salomon raised the money, and Washington defeated the British at Yorktown in the final battle of the war.

Salomon came through once more for his country—but his country did not come through for him.

Dying Broke

Haym Salomon died on January 6, 1785, barely two years after the treaty between Britain and the United States was signed. The government owed him money, which it never paid him. The man who was perhaps the cleverest financial genius of the Revolutionary War era died in bankruptcy— just the way his adopted country began its existence.

DEBORAH SAMPSON

Plympton, Massachusetts
December 17, 1760—April 29, 1827
Deserved a Chestful of Purple Hearts

Deborah Sampson, serving under the name of Robert Shurtleff, was one of the few women to serve as a combat soldier in the Continental Army. She paid a major price for her participation. Deborah was wounded in her first battle and never recovered fully. Nor was she compensated for her service until later in life. But, she soldiered on, happy to do what she could for her country.

Living a Life of Servitude

Deborah Sampson's early life was difficult. Her family was as poor as her opportunities for education, especially after her father drowned in a shipwreck in 1765. (Some accounts say he abandoned the family; either way, she and her five siblings were left without a father.) Deborah was indentured to a family named Thomas for eight years, starting at age ten.

When Deborah was released from her servitude in 1778, she had acquired enough education to become a schoolteacher, but she was too restless to follow that route. There was a war in progress and Deborah wanted to be a part of it. She did not see much future in rolling bandages for the army, the role commonly assigned to women. Deborah wanted to be a soldier. She had the physical and mental attributes—and the determination—required to enlist.

> ### REVOLUTIONARY REVELATIONS
> Deborah Sampson was about 5'8" tall, heavy boned, and strong, with a light complexion. Even her mother had a hard time picking her out once she donned her soldier's uniform.

Deborah Joins the Army

The Continental Army did not allow women to serve during the Revolutionary War. That did not stop Deborah. She tried to enlist as Robert Shurtleff of Carver, Massachusetts, early in 1782, selecting the name out of respect to her deceased brother. But she suspected that the recruiters recognized her as a woman because of the dainty way she held her quill pen. She failed to appear the next day for induction. Deborah tried again on May 20, 1782, in Uxbridge, where Noah Taft was forming a muster. This time she was successful. "Robert Shurtleff" was assigned to the Light Infantry Company of the Fourth Massachusetts Regiment, commanded by Captain George Webb. It was not long before her unit was in action.

> ### REVOLUTIONARY REVELATIONS
> The First Baptist Church of Middleborough, Massachusetts, excommunicated Deborah after her unit left Massachusetts because of a strong suspicion that she was "dressing in man's clothes and enlisting as a Soldier in the Army."

Fighting the British—and Detection

The regiment marched off to West Point to protect the area from the British still occupying New York City, fifty-five miles south. Skirmishes between the two sides were common. Deborah's first taste of combat came at Tappan Zee on July 3, 1782, where she reportedly fought well but sustained serious wounds. Two musket balls dug into her thigh and a British soldier scraped his saber across the left side of her head. She refused to go to a hospital, lest her gender be discovered. Good Samaritans transported her to one nonetheless.

Sampson had to be on guard constantly to protect her identity. Once, she was caught with a group of soldiers who grew suspicious of her behavior among them. Another time she was altering her uniform when comrades commented on her skill with a needle. She explained that there were no girls in her family, so "he" had to learn how to do his own sewing.

She used her ingenuity to escape detection. Deborah showed the surgeon her scalp wound, rather than the musket balls. He released her, and she tried to dig out the musket balls with her pen knife and a sewing needle. She could not extract both. She dug one out, but the other ball became embedded permanently.

Love Proves to Be Deborah's Undoing

Life got a little easier for Deborah once the Fourth Massachusetts was transferred to Philadelphia after the Treaty of Paris was signed. She was assigned to be General John Patterson's orderly. But health problems tripped her up. A fever rendered her unconscious and forced her into the hospital. Barnabas Binney, the doctor who treated her, discovered her secret.

Sampson pleaded with Dr. Binney not to tell anyone. He agreed, and moved her to his house for privacy and further treatment. Unfortunately, his niece fell in love with Robert Shurtleff. Sampson's deception unraveled.

Dr. Binney told General Patterson about Deborah. Patterson told General Henry Knox, who advised General Washington. The general confusion resulted in Robert Shurtleff's discharge from the Continental Army.

General Knox signed Shurtleff/Sampson's honorable discharge on October 25, 1783. General William Shepard, Colonel Henry Jackson, and General Patterson presented letters of commendation regarding her bravery.

Separation, Marriage, and Death

After a year and a half of service to her country, Robert Shurtleff was a free woman. For a while after her discharge, she traveled around New England and New York presenting lectures about her experiences in the military to raise some money. She wore the military uniform during her lectures, which always excited the audience. She returned to Massachusetts and married Benjamin Gannet on April 7, 1785. They had three children and adopted a fourth. She finally took up teaching to earn some money, which she needed badly.

Deborah was in debt for several years. That prompted her to exercise the same determination that had gotten her into the army in order to be paid in full for her service.

The army held back some of Sampson's pay after her discharge. She petitioned the state of Massachusetts and the U.S. Congress for back pay and a pension, becoming the first woman to ever apply for a military pension. Eventually, she received compensation and a pension.

Quotations to Live (and Die) By!

"[DEBORAH SAMPSON] EXHIBITED AN EXTRAORDINARY INSTANCE OF FEMALE HEROISM BY DISCHARGING THE DUTIES OF A FAITHFUL GALLANT SOLDIER, AND AT THE SAME TIME PRESERVING THE VIRTUE AND CHASTITY OF HER SEX, UNSUSPECTED AND UNBLEMISHED."

—THE GENERAL COURT OF MASSACHUSETTS

Finally, age and ill health caught up with Sampson. She died of yellow fever. Her legacy was commendable, though. She exemplified the ferocity and patriotism with which the colonists fought for their freedom, regardless of gender.

The country could never forget Deborah Sampson, and she never forgot the war. She had a constant reminder. When Deborah Sampson died, she still had that musket ball in her thigh—forty-five years later.

ROGER SHERMAN

Newton, Massachusetts
April 19, 1721–July 23, 1793
A Self-Made Man

Roger Sherman's lack of a formal education did not inhibit his political prospects. He went from making shoes to surveying land to justice of the peace, the Continental Congress, delegate to the Constitutional Convention, and U.S. senator. One of his notable achievements was signing the Declaration of Independence. And he helped build the population of the United States. He and his two wives produced fifteen children, almost enough to fill a congress of their own.

No Books? Write Your Own

There were not many opportunities for Roger Sherman to acquire a formal education in his hometown of Stoughton, Massachusetts. Fortunately, his father, a farmer of modest means, possessed a well-stocked library, and a local Harvard-trained minister, Reverend Samuel Dunbar, tutored him in mathematics, science, literature, and philosophy. Sherman's educational training was helpful, but he was not a "learned man" according to the standards of the time.

The town of Stoughton opened a public school when Roger was thirteen years old, which he attended for a while. He spent a good part of his youth apprenticed to a shoemaker. He was less than dedicated to the trade. He kept an open book in front of him most of the time. Reading became more of an occupation for him than making footwear.

After Sherman's father died in 1741, Roger moved to the rural, reading material–deprived town of New Milford, Connecticut, where his brother lived.

That didn't stop Sherman. The ever-resourceful young man wrote and published an almanac every year from 1750 to 1761 to alleviate the shortage of reading material in New Milford.

It did not take long before the people in the area recognized that he was a math and astronomy whiz and a budding political powerhouse.

For Land's Sake

New Haven County, Connecticut, needed a surveyor. The local government appointed Sherman to the post. From there it was a simple step to earn entry to the state bar when one of Sherman's neighbors asked him to assist a local lawyer working with a surveying-related petition at the county court. The lawyer reviewed Sherman's notes, which he found so precise that he encouraged the young surveyor to start his own law practice.

Next, Roger and his brother opened a store. That was the perfect place for Roger to act as town clerk. And, the local folks said, if he was town clerk he might as well represent the town at the Connecticut Provincial Assembly.

The members of the Assembly were duly impressed with Sherman. They appointed him as the colony's commissary for its troops.

As he took on more assignments, it was a safe prediction that his peers

FEDERAL FACTS

Even though he had an affinity for the military, Roger Sherman firmly opposed the 1775 appointment of George Washington as commander in chief of the Continental Army, as did many other New Englanders. They argued that the army at that time was from New England, had a satisfactory general of its own, and was doing a good job fighting the British.

would look to him to serve as a representative at the Continental Congress, where he served from 1774–81 and 1783–84. His hard work and willingness to take on new tasks were legendary at the meetings, as was his religious fervor, which caught his peers by surprise on occasion.

Sherman objected at times to meeting on the Sabbath, particularly when he thought the occasion did not require it. This is where he deviated slightly from the Founding Fathers. Sherman was willing to let the revolution wait while he prayed. His comrades wanted to declare independence first and thank God later. Fortunately, the delegates to Congress signed the Declaration of Independence on a Friday, so he was front and center to affix his name to the document.

FEDERAL FACTS

Roger Sherman was a member of the committee appointed to write a draft of the Declaration of Independence. Besides Sherman, the committee included Thomas Jefferson, Benjamin Franklin, John Adams, and Robert Livingston. Their first decision was to assign the job to. Jefferson, which he accepted. Even though Sherman signed the Declaration of Independence, he passed up a chance to help write it.

Call for Roger Sherman

Sherman worked tirelessly in Congress during the Revolutionary War. He served on numerous committees, but devoted much of his attention to local matters in New Haven, Connecticut, where he had moved in 1761. He served as the mayor of the city from 1784 to 1793, the year he died, and as a judge on the Connecticut Superior Court. While serving on the court he helped rewrite the entire state legal code.

Naturally, when Connecticut was looking for someone to represent it at the Constitutional Convention in 1787, Sherman's name came up.

A large number of the delegates to the convention were not happy with all the provisions the proposed document contained. They saw the need for a constitution, however.

Roger Sherman went to the convention with an open mind. He was among the delegates who held their noses and voted to ratify the Constitution, despite its shortcomings—many of which were rectified with the passage of the Bill of Rights. In fact, it was his proposal, known as the Connecticut Compromise, that was responsible for the creation of the current two-body federal legislature that is in place today.

Sherman's hardest job was convincing his fellow delegates from Connecticut that the document should be ratified. He used his persuasive powers to make sure they supported it. The state delegates did, by a majority of eighty-eight votes (128–40). Sherman's name was in the "yea" column.

There was one more office to come for Roger Sherman. He was named as a U.S. Senator in 1791. He was seventy years old at the time, and the constant wear and tear on his body was beginning to tell. He died of typhoid in 1793. The fever stilled one of the fledgling republic's most supportive voices.

THOMAS SUMTER

Hanover, Virginia
August 14, 1734–June 1, 1832
Woe Betide Anyone Who Burns Sumter's House

Sumter demonstrated to Americans that aggressive and innovative military leadership could win a war, even with occasional setbacks. He was well prepared for his military leadership role in South Carolina due to his experience fighting Indians in the mid-1700s. What he learned helped him prepare for leadership during the Revolutionary War and the multitude of political positions he held afterwards.

What Have You Done for Me Lately?

Sumter did not receive a formal education as a youth but his sense of adventure got him a long way. He began his military career in 1755, when he participated in the ill-fated Braddock Expedition.

In 1755, during the French and Indian War, the British initiated a campaign led by General Edward Braddock to capture a French stronghold, Fort Duquesne (modern Pittsburgh, Pennsylvania). It was a disaster. Braddock was killed, the British retreated in disgrace—and Sumter got his first taste of war.

Six years later, then-sergeant Sumter was involved in another expedition that gave him a chance to travel. He accompanied Henry Timberlake on a foray to the Virginia backcountry (in present-day Tennessee) to make sure the Cherokees had stopped fighting the settlers.

Sumter borrowed the money to buy a canoe and supplies for what was expected to be a short trip. Their timing was off. They left on November 28, 1761, to explore an area that was prone to wintry weather. Rivers ran low and froze, their unattended canoe slipped away while Sumter and Timberlake explored an icy cave, supplies ran out, Timberlake's luggage was looted—pretty much everything that could go wrong went wrong— but the men survived. A Cherokee chief, Ostenaco, expressed a desire to visit London and meet the king. Sumter and Timberlake accompanied him to England in May 1762. They met King George III and socialized with poets (Oliver Goldsmith), painters (Joshua Reynolds), and princes. Sumter, who was broke, asked the South Carolina government for a loan to repay the money he had laid out for his travel expenses. Officials denied it. Later, he entered debtors' prison in Virginia for nonpayment of an old debt. Going to jail gave Sumter a chance to exhibit his honesty. Joseph Martin, a friend of his, visited Sumter in the prison and gave him ten guineas and a tomahawk. With that money, Sumter bought his way out of jail in 1766. He repaid Martin—thirty years later.

In 1767 Sumter married a widow, Mary Jameson. The two worked hard and amassed a small fortune. He became a Provincial congressman and used some of the money to form his own militia, which proved to be a wise investment when the Revolutionary War began.

War, Not Politics

Once the fighting began, Sumter was front and center. He preferred military activity to politics. The young warrior was elected lieutenant colonel of the Second Regiment of the South Carolina Line in February 1776. He worked his way up to colonel and then brigadier general of the South Carolina militia, which was folded eventually into the Continental Army. Whatever his rank was, he engaged in numerous battles early in the war.

REVOLUTIONARY REVELATIONS

The British learned quickly who the feisty Thomas Sumter was. One British general noted that Sumter "fought like a gamecock." "Gamecock" became his nickname from that point on. General Charles Cornwallis, who left the Carolinas for Virginia due in part to Sumter's fighting prowess, described him as his greatest plague.

Sumter spread himself out across South Carolina. One of the first actions in which he participated was near Charleston, South Carolina, at the Battle of Sullivan's Island on June 28, 1776. There, the Americans defeated the British and sent them back to New York.

The peripatetic Sumter fought against Cherokees in the fall of 1776, against the British as they attempted to conquer Georgia via St. Augustine, Florida, and at Rocky Mount, South Carolina.

REVOLUTIONARY REVELATIONS

Sumter's military leadership reputation suffered a blow at Rocky Mount. The patriots attacked and defeated the enemy. Then Sumter's soldiers ripped into the enemy's stores, drank their liquor, and fell into drunken stupors. The British counterattacked and drove off the patriots.

One of the last battles in which Sumter fought was at Hanging Rock, South Carolina, on August 6, 1780. His troops attacked the Prince of Wales's American Regiment, composed of American Tories and supporting British units. Sumter's troops decimated the regiment, although the outcome of the battle was a draw. The patriots gained a sense of satisfaction because of the damage they inflicted on the Tory troops. For Sumter, it was a fitting farewell from the war.

Sumter then took a leave of absence from the Continental Army due to illness. The British burned and looted his home in 1780. After that, he rejoined the militia and set off on a vendetta against the British. He raised troops by promising each new recruit a slave, a horse, and the right to keep what he liberated (a.k.a. stole). That was too much for the governor, who vetoed Sumter's promise.

Things did not always go the way Sumter planned them after his return to the battlefield. He suffered an embarrassing defeat at Fishing Creek on August 18, 1780, when British General Banastre Tarleton caught Sumter's forces by surprise and routed them, even though the British were outnumbered almost four to one.

It was a humiliating setback for Sumter. He got revenge later that year at Blackstock's, on November 20, a battle in which the British suffered ten casualties to each one incurred by the patriots. Sumter was wounded in the back and chest that day. By this time, Sumter was operating more or less on his own, using guerilla-style tactics successfully. His hit-and-run attacks wore the British down.

The war in the South was wearing down, though, and Sumter's military career was over once General Cornwallis pulled up stakes and moved north in 1781.

FEDERAL FACTS
In between the battles in 1780, South Carolina Governor Edward Rutledge promoted Sumter to brigadier general. He was the last surviving general of the war.

From General to Senator

The people of South Carolina were kind to Sumter after the war. He would have preferred to stay on his plantation in Statesburg raising horses, which was a passion of his. But he accepted positions in the U.S. House of Representatives (1789–93, 1797–1801) and U.S. Senate (1801–10). That ended his public career.

Sumter lived for the next twenty-two years in well-earned privacy. He and his fellow South Carolina military leaders had shown that aggressiveness and innovative tactics could win battles—and ultimately a war. Sumter, like the country, had suffered a few setbacks along the way, but that was to be expected in a fight for independence.

BENJAMIN TALLMADGE

Brookhaven or Setauket, New York
February 25, 1754 – March 7, 1835
Spymaster

Yale graduate Benjamin Tallmadge was the superintendent of the high school at Wethersfield, Connecticut, when the Revolutionary War began. The fever of rebellion burning in so many patriots in the early 1770s afflicted him after the battles of Lexington and Bunker Hill. He joined the army in 1776 and set up the "Culper Ring," a group of spies, to keep General Washington apprised of British movements in and around New York City. He operated in secrecy, while many of his friends worked openly to defy the British. His undercover role was what made him so valuable to the American cause—and set him apart from his fellow patriots.

Loss of a Brother

Like so many of his fellow patriots, Tallmadge was from a middle-class background. His father was a Presbyterian minister, and there was nothing special about the young man's upbringing. By the time he graduated from Yale in 1773, the country was on the brink of war. Once the fighting began, he joined the army.

Extensive training was not an option for young soldiers in the 1770s. They enlisted one day and fought the enemy in the next battle. That was the case with Tallmadge. He received a commission as a lieutenant dated June 20, 1776, and engaged in the Battle of Long Island on August 27 that year. He was willing to do anything for the cause—especially after his brother died.

One of the Americans captured by the British at the battle of Long Island was Tallmadge's oldest brother William. The manner of his death infuriated Benjamin—he was starved to death, and the British did not allow any visitors to relieve his suffering. The cruelty and grief provided him with a personal incentive to defeat the British.

FEDERAL FACTS

The Battle of Long Island was the first major meeting of British and American troops after the Declaration of Independence was signed. It also turned out to be the largest single battle of the war, and a significant victory for the British.

The Culper Ring

After the Battle of Long Island ended, the newly promoted Major Benjamin Tallmadge transferred to the Second Dragoons. The unit fought up and down the East Coast for the rest of the war. They were especially busy during 1777. By mid-1778 they were back in the New York City area, and Tallmadge began a new career.

In 1778, General Washington asked Tallmadge to provide intelligence for the Continental Army about British operations around New York City. Tallmadge responded by setting up the Culper Ring, the most successful group of spies on either side in the Revolutionary War.

Tallmadge sought some trustworthy people who would be willing to place their lives on the line to help the patriots' cause. He visited Setauket, Long Island, and recruited a group of his childhood friends to conduct covert operations behind British lines on Long Island. From that point, the British found it difficult to make a move near New York City without a spy reporting on their activities.

Tallmadge realized that secret agents could not operate under their own names. He adopted the name John Bolton. One of his operatives, Abraham Woodhull, became Samuel Culper Sr. A third member, Robert Townsend, who joined the group later, assumed the moniker Samuel Culper Jr.

FEDERAL FACTS

Even though Tallmadge became one of the Continental Army's premier spies during the Revolutionary War, one of his classmates at Yale was less successful. That was Nathan Hale, whom the British hanged on September 22, 1776, for spying.

Eye Spy

The Culper Ring set up an elaborate network to uncover and transmit information to General Washington. Woodhull gathered information and observed British naval operations. He compiled reports he thought would interest Washington. Then, he gave dispatches to Caleb Brewster.

Caleb Brewster was particularly daring. He operated a fleet of whaleboats on Long Island Sound, which gave him access to several ports in the area. The British knew he was a spy, but that did not deter him from slipping in and out of places under their noses and collecting information about their operations.

Brewster carried the dispatches across Long Island Sound to Fairfield, Connecticut, and turned them over to Tallmadge. He, in turn, delivered them to General Washington.

Woodhull always felt as if he was one step away from being captured, so in 1779 he recruited a prominent New York City merchant, Robert Townsend, to act as the ring's primary agent there. Townsend provided significant services to the operation.

The Culper Ring operated for five years without detection, although its activities tailed off after 1780. Some of the information it uncovered paid off handsomely.

In 1780, members thwarted British plans to ambush the newly arrived French army in Rhode Island. That same year it helped unravel the plot between British intelligence officer Major John André and Benedict Arnold to turn the American fort at West Point, New York, over to the British army, although historians are at odds about their actual role in doing so.

Tallmadge's spy activities did not interfere with his military obligations. He continued to lead his troops in battle, including members of his ring. Caleb Brewster fought with Tallmadge in November 1780, when American troops captured Fort St. George at Mastic, New York.

REVOLUTIONARY REVELATIONS

Tallmadge was a faithful ringleader during and after the war. To the end, he would not reveal who the members were—not even to George Washington.

Life in Litchfield

After the war, Tallmadge settled down in Litchfield, Connecticut. He became the town's postmaster in 1792, and a successful banker and merchant.

Tallmadge served in the U.S. House of Representatives from 1801–17 as a Federalist, where he butted heads often with his fellow revolutionaries turned political opponents, particularly the Democratic-Republicans Jefferson and Madison.

By the time he died in 1835, he was retired from politics and business— and was living life completely in the open.

JAMES THACHER

Barnstable, Massachusetts
1754–1844
One Significant Contribution

James Thacher was twenty-one years old and just out of medical school when he began treating Revolutionary War soldiers in 1775. He is best known for his writings, including an 1823 military journal which revealed valuable information about the quality—or lack thereof—of medical facilities and treatment available to soldiers during the war. Harvard and Dartmouth presented him with honorary master of arts and doctor of medicine degrees, and the American Academy of Arts and Sciences named him a fellow. He wasn't always a popular "fellow" with his colleagues, though. He was sometimes outspoken and critical of American medical services during the war, which is something historians tend to overlook.

Quacks Need Not Apply

After James Thacher finished medical school in mid-1775, he apprenticed to the Cape Cod physician Abner Hersey, one of the early members of the Massachusetts Medical Society. Thacher was barely of legal age when he became a doctor in the Continental Army.

Even though the Continental Army did not give soldiers' medical treatment a high priority at the beginning of the Revolutionary War, it did apply strict criteria to the selection of doctors. In Thatcher's selection group, sixteen candidates for assignments as doctors with the

Continental Army assembled for their entrance exams in early July 1775. They appeared for four hours in front of a board for examination. Board members grilled them about four subjects: anatomy, physiology, surgery, and medicine. Only ten of the candidates were accepted. The others were rejected as being unqualified.

Thacher cleared the qualifying hurdle and earned acceptance into the army's medical corps. He was appointed to a post as a surgeon's mate in the provincial hospital in Cambridge, Massachusetts, where John Warren was the senior surgeon. Thacher looked at that as a benefit, because of Warren's excellent reputation and his compassionate care of the soldiers.

Thacher started working on July 15 in "hospitals." They were really large private homes in Cambridge which were open to accommodate the soldiers who had been wounded at Breed's (Bunker) Hill or contracted one of the various diseases that ravaged them and the population in general at the time. As bad as the hospitals were in 1775, they got worse as the fighting intensified.

FEDERAL FACTS
Smallpox, which John Adams said was "ten times more terrible than Britons, Canadians, and Indians together," killed more people than bullets during the Revolutionary War.

Thacher did not stay in Cambridge long. Later, he participated in the expedition of Ticonderoga and at the siege of Yorktown. Thacher witnessed the surrender of General Cornwallis and the execution of Major John André before retiring from army service in 1783 and settling in Plymouth, Massachusetts. During his eight-year enlistment, he produced some intriguing observations.

Descriptive, If Not Educational

Thacher's written contributions did not reveal any major medical milestones. Rather, they gave vivid pictures of hospitals, doctors, and treatments at the time. Thacher had the opportunity to work with Dr. Jonathan Potts, who managed the army's northern department of medical services. Potts, like so many other department heads, was overworked, understaffed, and poorly supplied.

> ### REVOLUTIONARY REVELATIONS
> Thacher was a hard worker. At the hospitals in Saratoga in 1777, he cared for patients daily from 8 A.M. to late evening. Generally, he had twenty wounded men under his care at any one time.

Because Thacher spent so much time working with wounded soldiers, he had little time for research, which was not unusual as the war progressed. Whatever new techniques or treatments he applied were learned through repetition, practice, and osmosis.

Very few doctors had a chance to do any innovative research during the war, since the demands on their time limited their abilities to find new ways to treat sick and wounded soldiers. They did what they could. Thacher simply reported on their endeavors, rather than contribute significantly to research efforts.

Among his observations, Thacher alluded to the fact that the medical community had not made any groundbreaking inroads into treating disease or illness six years into the war in an April 20, 1781, journal entry. He commented that 187 soldiers in his regiment had contracted smallpox. Worse, he noted, the lack of food hindered any treatment.

The military medical community was unhappy with the perpetual shortage of food and supplies at its disposal throughout the war. Men like Thacher and Benjamin Rush did their best with what they had.

After the War

When the war ended, Thacher returned to Massachusetts and established a private practice. He had not distinguished himself from other military surgeons with whom he had served. His most significant contribution came forty years later.

Thacher busied himself with his medical practice and civic projects in his hometown of Plymouth. In 1796, he and his brother-in-law, Dr. Nathan Hayward, established the first stagecoach line between Plymouth and Boston. Thacher introduced the tomato plant and the use of anthracite coal in Plymouth.

Like his mentor, Dr. Hersey, Thacher became a member of the Massachusetts Medical Society. His willingness to adopt new ideas and advance ideas that most of his peers had not even considered made him one of the most respected members of the association.

He wrote several books, including *Observations on Hydrophobia* (1812), *A Practical Treatise on the Management of Bees* (1829), and *An Essay on Demonology, Ghosts, Apparitions and Popular Superstitions*. His military journal became Thacher's biggest contribution to the history of the Revolutionary War.

James Thacher's name may never be mentioned in the same breath with John Adams, George Washington, Thomas Jefferson, or other Founding Fathers, but he did make that one significant contribution to the lore of the war. That was all it took to preserve his memory.

GEORGE WALTON

Walton, a successful lawyer in Georgia, was a political neophyte in 1776 when Georgia sent its somewhat dysfunctional trio of representatives to the Continental Congress in Philadelphia. Walton held the distinction of being one of the youngest signers of the Declaration of Independence, if not the youngest.

Glad You Could Make It

George Walton's parents died when he was an infant. (The exact year of his birth is unknown. Some sources list it as 1741, others as 1749. Either way, he was fairly young when he signed the document.) An uncle, who discouraged Walton from pursuing book learning, raised him. Nevertheless, the determined young man attended public schools in his native Virginia, and apprenticed as a carpenter. There was no better trade for building a nation, which Walton helped accomplish.

Most importantly, he was known for his anti-British politics and the pro-independence pamphlets he wrote. He had an impressive background in Georgia, where he had been elected to its Provincial Congress in 1775 and served as a member and president of the Committee of Intelligence. He was also a member and later president of the Council of Safety in 1775.

Still, he was unprepared for what he encountered when he arrived in Philadelphia. He was like the proverbial fish out of water compared

248

to the better educated delegates to the Second Continental Congress in Philadelphia.

There was so little coordination among the three Georgia delegates—Walton, Lyman Hall, and Button Gwinnett—that they traveled separately and arrived at different times. They almost did not arrive in time for the voting. Walton, Hall, and Gwinnett may have arrived in Philadelphia in the middle of the day, but they were completely in the dark about what was going on. The Congress was in no hurry to vet them. Even though Walton's selection as a delegate to the Congress was effective as of January 1776, he did not arrive in Philadelphia until late June. It was not until July 1 that the Secretary of the Congress approved his credentials certifying that he had been duly elected to Congress and had the right to serve. (Every delegate to the Congress had to present such credentials before they were seated and could participate on committees and vote.)

Arrived in Philadelphia, Left to Sign

Walton, Hall, and Gwinnett put aside their differences in Philadelphia and eventually agreed with the delegates from the other colonies that signing the Declaration of Independence would be good for America. They caused a bit of consternation before the final vote.

As of July 2, 1776, most of the colonies were in accord with the Declaration of Independence as written, with a few minor differences. Neither Georgia nor South

★ ★ ★ ★ ★ ★ ★ ★ ★ ★ ★ ★ ★

FEDERAL FACTS

Even though they had arrived in Philadelphia too late to participate fully in discussions about independence or contribute in a meaningful way to the writing of the final document, all three Georgia delegates signed the final draft of the Declaration of Independence. Their names are placed conspicuously on the left edge of the document, where they are almost as prominent as John Hancock's in the middle. George Walton was the last of three to sign.

Carolina wanted the clause abolishing slavery included in it. The delegates from the two colonies succeeded in getting it removed. That opened the door to the ultimate signing of the declaration.

A copy of the Declaration of Independence arrived in Savannah, Georgia, on August 8, 1776. Archibald Bulloch, Georgia's president of the Council of Safety, read it to a happy gathering of citizens two days later. The three signers from Georgia were heroes to the patriots and traitors to the British. That could have cost Walton his life—but did not.

Walton's Wild Ride after Philadelphia

Walton stayed in Philadelphia until October 1777. He returned to Georgia to fight the British as a soldier. His militia unit became engaged along the state's borders, particularly near Florida, to protect the colony from Indians. Walton was in Savannah when the British attacked it in December 1778. He was wounded and taken prisoner. The British captured and held him for two years. Finally, they exchanged him for a British naval officer. Even though he had signed the Declaration of Independence, which technically made him a traitor to the British crown, the British did not hold it against him.

Walton was not about to let a wound and a two-year incarceration slow him down. Once the British released him, he roamed the backwoods of Georgia encouraging the residents to continue the fight. The exposure paid off handsomely for him. Walton was reelected to the Continental Congress, where he served from 1780–81.

After the war ended, Walton was in great demand. He served as a commissioner to negotiate a treaty with the Cherokees in Tennessee in 1783 and became the chief justice of Georgia from 1783–89. During that period he was also a member of the Augusta Board of Commissioners in 1784–85 and represented Georgia in the settlement of the boundary line between South Carolina and Georgia in 1786. There did not seem to be an end to political opportunities in Georgia for Walton.

REVOLUTIONARY REVELATIONS

Walton was elected as a delegate to the convention to frame the federal Constitution in 1787. He declined the opportunity for unspecified reasons.

Walton was selected as governor of Georgia in 1789 by the state assembly and was appointed the first judge of the Superior Courts of the eastern judicial circuit in 1790. Then, he was appointed in 1795 to the United States Senate to fill the vacancy caused by the resignation of James Jackson. He served for three months, from November 16, 1795, to February 20, 1796, when a successor was elected. George Walton was the last of the dysfunctional Georgia delegation to the Continental Congress to die. Dysfunctional they might have been, but they showed exceptional unity when they signed the Declaration of Independence together.

JOSEPH WARREN

Roxbury, Massachusetts
June 11, 1741–June 17, 1775
An Incendiary Man

Dr. Joseph Warren, a close associate of prominent Massachusetts radicals such as John Hancock and Samuel Adams, is not as well known as them because he died so early in the Revolutionary War. Warren, who came from a family of patriots, is best known for two exploits: inspiring Paul Revere's ride, and dying in the line of duty at Bunker Hill. Neither one receives a great deal of publicity.

A Radical Doctor

Warren was a serious student in his younger days. He studied at the elite Roxbury Latin School and Harvard, from which he graduated in 1759. Following graduation, he taught at Roxbury Latin for a year, then studied medicine. Politics and independence were always on his mind, however.

Warren drew British authorities' attention to himself as early as 1768, when they threatened to try his publishers, Edes and Gill, for printing a hostile newspaper essay he had written under his pseudonym, "A True Patriot." But no local jury would indict. Later, in February 1770, a loyalist customs service agent named Ebenezer Richardson, who was being harassed by a group of young boys, fired shots into the crowd, killing the young Christopher Seider. That incident led to the Boston Massacre eleven days later, after which there was no turning back for the patriots.

Like so many of his fellow radicals, Warren was particularly incensed at the Intolerable Acts. In fairness, the British did not make the acts effective immediately. They gave the colonists an opportunity to accept them. Instead, the colonists grew more defiant. That defiance eventually cost Warren his life.

Quotations to Live (and Die) By!

"SHOULD EUROPE EMPTY ALL HER FORCE WE'LL MEET HER IN ARRAY."

—JOSEPH WARREN, 1774, AFTER HEARING ABOUT THE INTOLERABLE ACTS

Politics over Practice

As the conflict between the British government and the patriots widened, Warren became more active in politics. His fellow agitators appointed him to the Boston Committee of Correspondence in 1773. He took his duties seriously. Twice in the 1773–75 timeframe he delivered speeches to commemorate the Boston Massacre. On the second occasion, in March 1775, he did so while Boston was teeming with British troops.

In addition to his duties on the Committee of Correspondence, Warren found time to draft the

FEDERAL FACTS

The Boston Committee of Correspondence resulted from a motion made by Samuel Adams at a town meeting on November 2, 1772. It comprised twenty-two men chaired by James Otis Jr. The committee's goal was to shape public opinion and disseminate to local and neighboring citizens the community's views about colonists' rights and real or perceived abuses by British officials. Eighty other Massachusetts communities formed similar committees within a few months.

Suffolk Resolves, a prelude to the Declaration of Independence, which the Continental Congress ultimately endorsed.

Warren also served as president of the Massachusetts Provincial Congress, which the patriots formed to bypass the British government's laws intended to strip them of self-rule. Ironically, the Congress ruled every community in Massachusetts except Boston, where most of the radicals lived. The British had too large a presence there.

> ## REVOLUTIONARY REVELATIONS
> Warren's brother James also served a term as president of the Massachusetts Provincial Congress, as did Samuel Adams. That was the highest position in the state's government at the time.

A Good Doctor Falls

Like so many of his compatriots, Warren put his life on the line as a politician and patriot. He took it one step farther than many of the other patriots. Warren also served in the military as a major general in the Massachusetts militia. Thus, when events spiraled out of control in April 1775, he was ready to sacrifice his life for the patriots' cause—which he did.

Warren was one of the last patriot leaders left in Boston in mid-1775. Many of them were en route to the Second Continental Congress in Philadelphia or hiding from the British in other towns. The British were determined to find them.

When the British sent a patrol to find and arrest John Hancock and Samuel Adams, who were "vacationing" in nearby Concord, Warren dispatched Paul Revere and William Dawes to alert the two men—an act that became legendary and was immortalized in Henry Wadsworth Longfellow's famous poem, "Paul Revere's Ride."

On April 19, 1775, British and American troops clashed at Lexington and Concord in the first battles of the Revolutionary War. Warren volunteered to fight at the Battle of Bunker Hill as a private—even though he outranked Colonel William Prescott, who was in actual command.

Joseph Warren died at Bunker Hill as he had lived: heroically. The British did not accord him any respect after his death, though. After the battle, British soldiers stripped Warren's body of his clothing and bayoneted him until he was unrecognizable. Then they shoved his remains into a shallow ditch. His brothers and Paul Revere exhumed his body ten months later.

Quotations to Live (and Die) By!

"THE FAMOUS DOCTOR WARREN, THE GREATEST INCENDIARY IN ALL AMERICA, WAS KILLED ON THE SPOT."
—BRITISH OFFICER LIEUTENANT LORD FRANCIS RAWDON

Abigail Adams lamented Warren's death. She wrote to John Adams on July 5, 1775, "We want him in the Senate; we want him in his profession; we want him in the field. We mourn for the citizen, the senator, the physician, and the warrior. May we have others raised up in his room."

MERCY OTIS WARREN

West Barnstable, Massachusetts
September 24, 1728–October 19, 1814
Drama Queen

Since Mercy Otis Warren could not carry a sword during the Revolutionary War, she wielded a pen, which was almost as lethal in her hands. She had an acute grasp of politics, particularly as they applied to the outcome of the war, which she expressed in plays, poems, pamphlets, and letters. Even though it was a man's world in the 1700s, men certainly recognized her value to their patriotic cause. She was a rarity for the time: a woman who was not shy about voicing her opinion in public about independence.

Education by Osmosis

Mercy was raised at a time when families were either fierce Tories or patriots. There was no in between. The Otis family was decidedly in the patriot camp.

Her father, James Otis Sr., was adamantly opposed to King George III's policies, and he was outspoken against Massachusetts' governor, Thomas Hutchinson. His feelings rubbed off on his three children.

Mercy Otis's father believed fervently in the value of a solid education, especially for his sons. That turned out to be an advantage for her. James Sr. hired the Reverend Jonathan Russell to tutor her brothers to prepare them for entry into Harvard. Reverend Russell allowed Mercy to sit in on his lessons and use his library. It was not a formal education for Mercy, but it gave her a background that she used later to needle the British and support the patriots.

Quotations to Live (and Die) By!

"TELL YOUR WIFE THAT GOD ALMIGHTY HAS ENTRUSTED HER WITH THE POWERS FOR THE GOOD OF THE WORLD, WHICH, IN THE CAUSE OF HIS PROVIDENCE, HE BESTOWS ON FEW OF THE HUMAN RACE. THAT INSTEAD OF BEING A FAULT TO USE THEM, IT WOULD BE CRIMINAL TO NEGLECT THEM."

—JOHN ADAMS IN A LETTER TO JAMES WARREN

Marriage did nothing to change Mercy's political views. In fact, it strengthened her patriotic fervor. She married her second cousin, James Warren (no relation to Joseph or John Warren), in 1754. As a result, she developed strong friendships with the anti-British leaders of the rebellion in Massachusetts—and their wives. One of the women with whom Mercy Warren was closest was the considerably younger Abigail Adams. She was both mentor and friend to Abigail.

The Warrens hosted many meetings of the radicals in their home. Noted leaders such as John Adams, Samuel Adams, and John Hancock sought her advice on what to do and how to do it. As a result, she became an activist, rather than just a listener, an unusual position for a woman at the time.

FEDERAL FACTS

James Warren served for a time as the Continental Army's paymaster. Even though he held the rank of general in the provincial militia, Warren did not participate actively in the war after the fighting ended in Massachusetts. He refused to serve under Continental Army officers of lesser rank.

The Pen Is Mightier Than the Sword

Mercy wrote a series of pamphlets, poems, and plays to stir the hearts and minds of the people of Massachusetts. One of her favorite targets was Governor Hutchinson, whom her father and brothers had criticized vocally for many years.

REVOLUTIONARY REVELATIONS

Mercy Warren wrote plays even though there were no theaters in Boston at the time. They were published in newspapers instead. Two prewar political satires in particular, *The Adulateur* (1773) and *The Group* (1775), caught the public's fancy.

Mercy was aware that she was upsetting many Tories because of her writings. That did not deter her. She also recognized the dangers the patriots faced by openly defying the British and all they could lose. The potential perils did not force her to stow her quill in the inkwell and leave it there.

Quotations to Live (and Die) By!

"BUT OH! THE DREAD OF LOSING ALL THAT THIS WORLD CAN BESTOW BY ONE COSTLY SACRIFICE KEEPS MY MIND IN CONTINUAL ALARMS."

—MERCY OTIS WARREN TO ABIGAIL ADAMS

Warren continued to write after the war ended and the country had settled down enough to concentrate on creating the Constitution and Bill of Rights. She published two poems in 1790, known collectively as "Poems Dramatic and Miscellaneous." They were "The Sack of Rome" and "The Ladies of Castile."

Mercy Otis Warren's best-known work was the three-volume *History of the Rise, Progress, and Termination of the American Revolution*, which she finished in 1805.

Warren started writing a history of the Revolutionary War while it was in progress, when the events were fresh in her mind. It was not a successful commercial venture for her. She was one of the few people who paid a price for the book.

Publication cost her the friendships of John and Abigail Adams, albeit temporarily, and upset friends and readers because of the way she portrayed some of the patriots.

 Quotations to Live (and Die) By!

"MR. ADAMS' PASSIONS AND PREJUDICES WERE SOME-TIMES TOO STRONG FOR HIS SAGACITY AND JUDGMENT."
—MERCY OTIS WARREN IN THE *HISTORY OF THE RISE, PROGRESS, AND TERMINATION OF THE AMERICAN REVOLUTION*

Mercy Has Her Doubts

Even though Mercy favored independence, she was not sold on the need for a U.S. Constitution. Neither was her husband. Warren resorted to her pen to campaign against the Constitution. She stated her objections in a 1788 document, *Observations on the new Constitution, and on the Federal and State Conventions*. Following the custom of the time, she signed it with a pen name, "A Columbian Patriot." For a time, people believed that it had been written by Elbridge Gerry.

Once she learned that her protests were being ignored, she campaigned to have equal rights for women included in the Constitution. That fell on deaf ears, too.

Quotations to Live (and Die) By!

"DEMOCRATIC PRINCIPLES ARE THE RESULT OF EQUAL-
ITY OF CONDITION."

—MERCY OTIS WARREN

Mercy's Last Few Years

Mercy's history book was her last significant publication. She continued her correspondence with friends and family between then and 1814,
when she died. One of her final achievements was to mend her rift with
John and Abigail Adams.

Mercy Otis Warren died at eighty-six. Death, however, did not silence
her voice. It is still being heard through her numerous writings two centuries later.

GEORGE WASHINGTON

Westmoreland County, Virginia
February 22, 1732–December 14, 1799
Four Bullets and Two Dead Horses

The name most often cited as the country's Founding Father is George Washington. He was a man of accomplishment, whose well-documented list of "firsts" established him as one of the pre-eminent Americans in the country's history. His military leadership enabled a raggedy Continental Army to defeat its professional British enemy. Then, when the United States was struggling to survive in the late 1780s, he stepped in to ensure passage of its new Constitution. Appreciative citizens elected him as their first president—then reelected him. He deserved the encomiums heaped on him, even though he might have been the first one to admit that he did not do the job alone. But he certainly played a leading role.

Early Days

It was a common practice among wealthy Virginians in the early 1700s to send their sons to England to receive an education. George Washington was an exception. He was trained as a surveyor. He spent a large part of his young adult years surveying Lord Thomas Fairfax's land in the Shenandoah Valley of Virginia and fighting Indians in the French and Indian War.

Washington honed his military leadership skills during that war, which served him in good stead in the years to come.

> ## REVOLUTIONARY REVELATIONS
>
> In 1755 George Washington served as an aide to General Edward Braddock in the ill-fated expedition to capture Fort Duquesne. During one skirmish, four bullets lodged in Washington's coat without injuring him, and two horses were killed as he rode them.

By 1759, Washington had had enough of surveying and fighting. He went home to Mount Vernon to tend to his lands in peace and marry Martha Dandridge Custis. His marriage was peaceful; his domestic life was not.

From Delegate to Commander in Chief

Washington could not ignore the British tax and legislative policies aimed at the colonies. As a member of the Virginia House of Burgesses, he was in a position to fight against them, which he did throughout the 1760s and early 1770s. The fight became literal in 1775.

Virginia elected George Washington as a delegate to the Second Continental Congress in 1775. His stay was short. He took his seat on May 10, 1775. On June 15, he walked out as the commander in chief of the Continental Army after John Adams urged Congress to appoint him to the post.

> ## REVOLUTIONARY REVELATIONS
>
> George Washington originally wanted to become an officer in the British army, but the British never offered him a commission. That was one of the little flukes of history that changed the direction of the world.

Even though Washington had never commanded anything larger than a regiment, he found himself in charge of an army of sorts. Leading it into battle was one thing; keeping it fed and supplied was another. That became his biggest challenge throughout the Revolutionary War, starting at the siege of Boston.

Washington had his ups and downs after he arrived in Boston on July 3, 1775, to take command. He suffered a series of losses early in the war that made the patriots wonder if he was indeed the right man for the job. Washington had to fight political battles in addition to military skirmishes, though more than anything he longed to be home at Mount Vernon with a life free of strife and war.

Washington survived all the hardships of the war and finally vanquished his British opponent by following a simple strategy: Avoid direct combat with the enemy whenever possible.

FEDERAL FACTS

On more than one occasion politicians and military leaders tried to remove Washington as commander in chief. One of the most salient attempts occurred in the 1777 Conway Cabal, when a group of civilian and army leaders tried to replace Washington with an Irishman, General Thomas Conway, who had less seniority than many other American commanders. The plot was uncovered and Washington's job was saved; so was the country.

Quotations to Live (and Die) By!

"WE SHOULD ON ALL OCCASIONS AVOID A GENERAL ACTION, OR PUT ANYTHING TO THE RISQUE, UNLESS COMPELLED BY A NECESSITY, INTO WHICH WE OUGHT NEVER TO BE DRAWN."
—GEORGE WASHINGTON TO CONGRESS

President Washington

Washington, like so many of his peers, was disappointed with the Articles of Confederation that had been drafted in 1776–77 as the nation's first Constitution. He came out of retirement in 1787 to oversee the national convention formed to write a new Constitution. Once again he got more than he had signed up for. In 1789 he was elected to the first of his two terms as president of the United States.

Washington's second stint as commander in chief—this time of a nation rather than an army—was no easier than his first. It was similar in one respect: The position required a great deal of on-the-job training.

One of the problems Washington experienced was the formation of an opposition party. He envisioned a strong republic governed by one independent party. But Jefferson helped form the Democratic-Republican Party, and Alexander Hamilton spearheaded the creation of the Federalist Party, which Washington supported but never joined officially.

Despite the emergence of the two-party system and the challenges it posed for his policies, Washington oversaw significant domestic and foreign growth for the United States during his two terms.

He kept the United States neutral in a war in Europe that began in 1793, opened western lands, initiated the construction of a national infrastructure, supported Alexander Hamilton's plans for a national bank and a viable system of taxation, issued the first presidential Thanksgiving proclamation . . . and that's just for starters.

Quotations to Live (and Die) By!

"[WASHINGTON] IS TOO ILLITERATE, UNREAD, UNLEARNED FOR HIS STATION AND REPUTATION."

—JOHN ADAMS

By the time Washington left office on March 4, 1797, he had set the United States on a course of stability and growth and created a foundation on which it could thrive. He earned his reputation as "First in war, first in peace, and first in the hearts of his countrymen"—although not everyone agreed.

Again, Washington retired. Again, his country called. His successor as president, John Adams, appointed him on July 4, 1798, as a lieutenant general and commander in chief "of the armies raised or to be raised for service in a prospective war." He served in that capacity until December 14, 1799—the day he died.

Washington's death left a void in the United States that was hard to overcome. The country erected a monument in his honor in Washington, D.C., that stands as a testimony to all he did to support the United States. His reputation as the "Father of His Country" is monument enough.

MARTHA WASHINGTON

Williamsburg, Virginia
June 2, 1731–May 22, 1802
Second Husband, First Lady

Martha Dandridge Custis Washington was a woman who loved life, despite the occasional heartbreaks that interrupted it. Even though her husband was hailed after his death as "First in war, first in peace, and first in the hearts of his countrymen," she had a unique first of her own: the first First Lady. Her life changed considerably after she married George Washington. She had to learn to live in military camps and function under the threat of kidnapping and set the precedent for how First Ladies are expected to act. She handled it all with aplomb.

Where There's No Will, There's a Way

Martha Dandridge enjoyed an advantage over the young ladies in her neighborhood early in her life. Her father made sure she received a basic education in mathematics, reading, and writing, which was not a common practice for young ladies at the time.

Her first husband, Daniel Parke Custis, died in 1757, leaving her with two young children. (Two others had died at young ages.) Custis died without a will, which left her with over 17,000 acres of land to manage. That, too, was uncommon. In Virginia in the 1750s, most wealthy men used to leave their estates and minor children in the hands of a guardian, who managed both—and the guardian was almost never their wives.

Daniel's death highlighted the value of Martha's early education, as basic as it was. With the help of her former husband's business managers and a few lawyers, Martha managed the estate efficiently.

But a large plantation was a lonely place for a twenty-six-year-old widow in the mid-1700s. Most young widows remarried in those times. She was not one to defy tradition. Martha married a young military officer named George Washington on January 6, 1759. They would remain husband and wife for forty years.

REVOLUTIONARY REVELATIONS

Actually, Martha was George's second choice. He was smitten with an attractive neighbor, Sally Fairfax. Sally married George Williams, so George settled for Martha Custis—and her estate.

Let George Do It

Both Martha and George benefited from their marriage. She gained a husband to help her manage the plantation. He gained the plantation that he helped manage. They also loved and respected one another. It was a perfect union—until the unpleasantness over British tax policies tore Virginia and the other colonies apart.

REVOLUTIONARY REVELATIONS

Martha Washington was only five feet tall. George Washington was six feet, two inches tall. Allegedly, she made up for their height difference when she wanted to get a point across to him by grabbing his shirt collar and pulling him down to her level.

The couple's finances took a hit in the 1760s due to uncertain economic conditions and the couple's penchant for hosting expensive parties. The parties and accompanying festivities occupied Martha's time. The economic conditions kept George busy on the political front. Before long he was involved on the military front as well.

REVOLUTIONARY REVELATIONS

George Washington was elected to represent Fairfax County in the Virginia House of Burgesses and served on local municipal and church boards and committees. It was a busy time for the Washingtons. For the most part, Martha stayed away from the politics of it all.

Winter Camp

In June 1775, the Continental Congress appointed George Washington as the commander in chief of an army that barely existed. That changed Martha's life dramatically.

There were rumors that Virginia's Royal Governor Dunmore would try to kidnap Martha to gain leverage against the general and the patriots. That placed added stress on her, although the kidnapping never took place.

As the war raged, Martha made it a practice to visit George every winter at his various camps. Her trips were marked by parades and parties all along the route as patriotic citizens thanked her for George's leadership on their behalf. She was leery of the attention at first, but she learned to live with it.

Martha performed her own patriotic deeds. She helped the Ladies of Philadelphia transfer money, clothing, and supplies directly to George Washington. And she recruited Thomas Jefferson's wife, also named Martha, to head a similar campaign in Virginia.

REVOLUTIONARY REVELATIONS

Martha Washington donated $20,000 of her own money to help finance the war.

During the war, Martha—who had in 1773 lost her third child—suffered another devastating setback. Her son from her first marriage, Jacky, died in October 1781 of fever while serving as a civilian aide to General Washington at the siege of Yorktown. She had never coped with the deaths of her loved ones particularly well. This time was no exception.

Despite the hardships caused by deprivation, travel, and separation, Martha and George survived the war with their lives and marriage intact. The next test of their marriage would be less severe, but just as demanding.

Life as First Lady

For a short while after the war, Martha and George returned to their home, Mount Vernon, to live what they hoped would be a normal family life. Once again, the country demanded George's services. He was elected president of the United States in 1789.

REVOLUTIONARY REVELATIONS

Martha Washington missed George's first inaugural ball, which was held before she could get to New York, the nation's temporary capital, from Virginia.

Martha's life became a whirlwind of activities. She moved from Mount Vernon to New York City to Philadelphia. Wherever she was, Martha dressed formally, received visitors, hosted parties, and visited leading members of society. She did whatever it took to make sure the presidential home was open and the right people were treated with respect.

One of the leading social dilemmas at the first capital was what to call the First Lady. Some people called her "Lady Washington." Others referred to her simply as "Lady Presidentess."

Once again the couple got through the difficult time on a "learn as you go" basis. They could not have done too badly: George was elected for a second term.

Finally, after eight years as president and "Lady Presidentess," George and Martha returned to Mount Vernon—but not for long. George died less than two years after he left office. Martha lived for two-and-a-half years beyond that.

REVOLUTIONARY REVELATIONS

Martha Washington did not attend George's funeral. She was too overcome with grief.

The nation may have suffered two great losses when Martha Washington died. The first was her death. The second was all the letters she and George had exchanged over the years, which may have contained some riveting historical information. She burned them all in March 1802.

Martha Washington also burned her own name into U.S. history. That will never be lost.

JOHN WITHERSPOON

East Lothian, Scotland

February 5, 1723–November 15, 1794

Committee Commando

John Witherspoon came to New Jersey from Scotland to turn the under-funded and poorly attended College of New Jersey (now Princeton University) into a first-rate school. Subsequently, he was elected to the New Jersey state legislature and the Continental Congress. Witherspoon was different from most of the patriots who supported the American Revolution: he was a non-native. He adopted his new home and supported wholeheartedly its fight for independence—at a severe personal price. His son, Major James Witherspoon, died of wounds incurred at the October 1777 Battle of Germantown. That was a price John Witherspoon was willing to pay, albeit brokenheartedly.

Anti-British by Nature

John Witherspoon, a prominent evangelical Presbyterian minister, lived—and preached—in Scotland. Benjamin Rush and Richard Stockton traveled from New Jersey in 1766 to invite Witherspoon to America as head professor and president at the Presbyterian College of New Jersey in Princeton. Initially, his wife Elizabeth was reluctant to travel overseas. She relented two years later, and the Witherspoons arrived in America soon thereafter.

It was not difficult for the colonists to win Witherspoon over to the cause of the patriots once he arrived in America. Since the Scottish and

English were never bosom buddies, it was a foregone conclusion that he would adopt an anti-British stance. But he was not involved heavily in politics in his early years in New Jersey. He had to resurrect the college first.

Witherspoon made some significant changes at Princeton. He upgraded the physical facilities, revamped the curriculum, improved the quality of the faculty, and did whatever he could do to bring the college on par with Yale and Harvard.

Witherspoon had his critics in his early days at Princeton, especially when it came to politics. Some of them accused him of turning the college into a "seminary of sedition."

Dealing with the criticism occupied his time for a while, but the growing interference by the British in American affairs and the concomitant influence of the Anglican Church bothered the staunch Presbyterian. He took the changes personally.

FEDERAL FACTS

James Madison, Aaron Burr, the incendiary writer Philip Freneau ("The Poet of the American Revolution"), and Hugh Henry Brackenridge, the Scottish-born writer, lawyer, judge, and justice of the Pennsylvania Supreme Court, were among Witherspoon's students at Princeton.

Witherspoon became heavily involved in the American fight for independence. He began working with the Committee of Correspondence and Safety in 1774. His dedication was recognized and he was elected to serve as a delegate to the Second Continental Congress in 1776, along with Richard Stockton and Francis Hopkinson. The previous delegates, who had resisted independence, were kept home.

Witherspoon was a rarity among the delegates to the Second Continental Congress. He was a Presbyterian, whereas most of the delegates from the north were Congregationalists, and those from the south were Episcopalians (Anglicans). And he was the only active member of the clergy—and the only college president—to sign the Declaration of

Independence. In that same year, Witherspoon attracted a lot more attention when one of his sermons, "The Dominion of Providence over the Passions of Men," was published widely.

Quotations to Live (and Die) By!

"I WILLINGLY EMBRACE THE OPPORTUNITY OF DECLARING MY OPINION WITHOUT ANY HESITATION, THAT THE CAUSE IN WHICH AMERICA IS NOW IN ARMS, IS THE CAUSE OF JUSTICE, OF LIBERTY, AND OF HUMAN NATURE."

—JOHN WITHERSPOON IN "THE DOMINION OF PROVIDENCE OVER THE PASSIONS OF MEN"

Chaplain and Champion

John Hancock appointed Witherspoon as the Congress's chaplain. Committee after committee benefited from his participation. In his time in Congress, Witherspoon served on more than one hundred committees.

Witherspoon was a meticulous delegate. As a late arrival to the Congress, he made sure he had all the facts at hand before voting for independence.

And when delegates argued about whether or not the country was ready for independence, he was quick to insist that it was, so they would not have to do Parliament's bidding.

Quotations to Live (and Die) By!

"IT IS A WISE MAXIM TO AVOID THOSE THINGS WHICH OUR ENEMIES WISH US TO PRACTICE."

—JOHN WITHERSPOON

On July 1, 1776, Adams presented an impassioned speech on behalf of independence, which he completed before the New Jersey contingent arrived. When Stockton, Hopkinson, and Witherspoon arrived, they demanded that he repeat the speech. Adams accommodated their request. It was only then that the New Jersey men said they were satisfied and ready for the question, which was then voted on in the affirmative.

Witherspoon's Later Service

The British extracted a price for Witherspoon's support of the Declaration of Independence. The British army set up camp at Princeton in November 1776. Witherspoon knew that damage to the school was a possibility. He closed the campus and sent the students away on November 1. His worst fears were realized. The British destroyed the main building on the campus, Nassau Hall, and Witherspoon's personal notes and papers. Continental Army troops also did their share of damage. An artillery unit commanded by Alexander Hamilton fired a round through a window in the campus prayer hall and destroyed a portrait of King George II. Even British army commanders were concerned about the misconduct among their soldiers in the New Jersey campaign, although they blamed the Hessians. Congress assigned a committee to look into the matter on January 16, 1777. Witherspoon was one of the seven members.

Witherspoon assumed the responsibility of rebuilding Nassau Hall after the war. That created a great deal of financial difficulty for him and affected his personal life as well. He was unable to rebuild his life as quickly as he could restore the damaged campus.

By 1794 the aging Witherspoon's health was deteriorating. He had lost sight in both eyes in separate accidents in the preceding two years. He died that year on his farm near Princeton. He never lost the belief that he had done the right thing by voting for American independence.

APPENDIX A

The Acts of King George III and Parliament

Three acts of King George and the British Parliament in particular were the primary reasons American colonists were up in arms in the mid-1700s: the Stamp Act of 1765, the Tea Act of 1773, and the Intolerable Acts of 1774.

The Stamp Act of 1765

The British government needed revenue to pay for the 1754–63 French and Indian War, a long-running conflict between France and Britain that spread to the American colonies. One way to get the money was to raise taxes on American colonists, since they benefited from the war. The result was the Stamp Act of 1765.

The British neglected to confer with the colonists before enacting the new law. The colonists, who objected to being taxed without representation, rebelled against King George III and Parliament. Their displeasure drew British retaliation in the form of the Intolerable Acts of 1774.

Quotations to Live (and Die) By!

"AN ACT FOR GRANTING AND APPLYING CERTAIN STAMP DUTIES, AND OTHER DUTIES, IN THE BRITISH COLONIES AND PLANTATIONS IN AMERICA, TOWARDS FURTHER DEFRAYING THE EXPENCES OF DEFENDING, PROTECTING, AND SECURING THE SAME; AND FOR AMENDING SUCH PARTS OF THE SEVERAL ACTS OF PARLIAMENT RELATING TO THE TRADE AND REVENUES OF THE SAID COLONIES AND PLANTATIONS, AS DIRECT THE MANNER OF DETERMINING AND RECOVERING THE PENALTIES AND FORFEITURES THEREIN MENTIONED."

—THE FIRST PARAGRAPH OF THE STAMP ACT OF 1765

The Tea Act of 1773

The British Parliament passed the Tea Act on May 10, 1773. Strangely enough, it was not designed to raise revenues in the American colonies. In fact, it did not levy any new taxes. Parliament's goal was to rescue a British business, the East India Company, which was experiencing financial difficulties, partly because it had eighteen million pounds of unsold tea in its inventory. Under the terms of the Tea Act, the company would ship the unsold tea directly to the colonies and sell it via British agents at a lower price than local merchants could. American political leaders suspected a plot. They believed that the Tea Act was a ploy to elicit popular support for the taxes already in place and undermine local merchants' business. Their opposition led to the Boston Tea Party.

The Intolerable Acts of 1774

The British government was not pleased with the colonists' sometimes violent reaction to the Stamp/Tea Acts. In response, it passed four punitive laws called the Intolerable Acts, which placed new regulatory burdens on the citizens of Massachusetts and increased their opposition to the king and Parliament. (A fifth law dealt with enlarging the borders of Quebec.)

The Intolerable Acts included the Boston Port Act (a ban on shipping or receiving goods within the harbor of Boston); the Administration of Justice Act (stronger enforcement of the laws aimed at rioters and other people who defied British law); the Massachusetts Government Act (which strengthened the powers of the government of the province of the Massachusetts Bay); the Quartering Act (which forced colonists to provide living quarters for British officers and soldiers in places where no barracks existed); and the Quebec Act (which expanded the province of Quebec and allowed Catholics in Quebec to practice their faith openly).

The sequence of events stemming from these acts led to famous events in American history such as the Boston Massacre, the Boston Tea Party, the Revolutionary War—and independence.

While most women could play only limited roles during the Revolutionary War era, some prominent women were able to achieve significant accomplishments in the cause of liberty. Two women's groups in particular, the Philadelphia Ladies Association and the Daughters of Liberty, were vocal about their support of independence for the country. These groups included prominent women such as Martha Washington, Sarah Franklin Bache (Benjamin Franklin's daughter), and Esther de Berdt Reed.

The Ladies Association of Philadelphia

There was never enough money or materiel to keep the American fighting forces supplied throughout the war. In 1780, several prominent ladies living in Philadelphia decided, after the fall of Charleston, South Carolina, to alleviate the shortages as much as they could. Esther de Berdt Reed was instrumental in forming the Philadelphia Ladies Association.

Esther de Berdt was born in London, England, on October 22, 1746. Later, she met Joseph Reed, an American who had studied law there and lived with her family. He became Washington's secretary and aide-de-camp and governor of Pennsylvania. She married him in 1769 and moved with him to Philadelphia shortly thereafter. Despite her English upbringing, she became highly supportive of the American independence movement.

Reed gathered some of the leading ladies of Philadelphia to collect as much money as possible to supplement what little General Washington could access after hearing about the American soldiers' dearth of supplies and food. The general was not enthusiastic about their support. His first reaction to the association's

FEDERAL FACTS

Continental Army General Benjamin Lincoln surrendered Charleston, South Carolina on May 12, 1780, after a six-week siege. The British captured approximately 5,000 American soldiers and a major port as a result. It was the largest loss of American troops during the Revolutionary War.

offer was "Thanks, but no thanks," even though he had once lamented to Joseph Reed that the shortage of funds would mean the loss of his army. On second thought, he relented. Washington asked the ladies to use the money they collected to make 1,000 shirts for the soldiers. That idea took hold. They made 2,200 shirts!

Quotations to Live (and Die) By!

"OUR AMBITION IS KINDLED BY THE SAME OF THOSE HEROINES OF ANTIQUITY, WHO HAVE RENDERED THEIR SEX ILLUSTRIOUS, AND HAVE PROVED TO THE UNIVERSE, THAT, IF THE WEAKNESS OF OUR CONSTITUTION, IF OPINION AND MANNERS DID NOT FORBID US TO MARCH TO GLORY BY THE SAME PATHS AS THE MEN, WE SHOULD AT LEAST EQUAL, AND SOMETIMES SURPASS THEM IN OUR LOVE FOR THE PUBLIC GOOD. I GLORY IN ALL THAT WHICH MY SEX HAS DONE GREAT AND COMMENDABLE."

—ESTHER REED, IN HER NEWSPAPER ARTICLE "THE SENTIMENTS OF AN AMERICAN WOMAN"

Reed's original plan was to raise money and turn it over to Martha Washington, who would then forward it to General Washington. Reed appointed herself treasurer of the association to facilitate the transfer.

The ladies used a unique approach for the time. They went door to door across the city for donations and supplies. The people of Philadelphia were happy to help, even if George Washington spurned it at first. Approximately 1,600 Philadelphians contributed.

Sew What?

The women heeded Washington's request and began sewing. They amassed a hefty amount of money to support their efforts. The association raised approximately $7,500 in the short time it was in existence (1780–1781).

Reed and her associates accomplished more than just sewing shirts. They established a precedent by bringing women together to support the independence movement and creating a place for them to gather without violating social norms imposed on them by contemporary standards. Their innovation encouraged women elsewhere to launch their own organizations.

Quotations to Live (and Die) By!

"THE BEST PATRIOT, THE MOST ZEALOUS AND ACTIVE, AND THE MOST ATTACHED TO THE INTERESTS OF HER COUNTRY."

—FRENCH SECRETARY OF LEGATION M. DE MARBOIS TO JOSEPH REED IN A LETTER COMMENDING ESTHER REED'S EFFORTS ON BEHALF OF HER ADOPTED COUNTRY

Sadly, Esther Reed did not live to see her idea evolve. She died of an unknown illness in Flemington, New Jersey, on September 18, 1780, where she and her six children had fled to evade British troops who were threatening to invade Philadelphia. Esther was thirty-four at the time.

Sarah Franklin Bache (1743–1808), Benjamin Franklin's only daughter, stepped in to assume the leadership of the Ladies Association and complete the project. Similar groups sprang up in Maryland, New Jersey, Virginia, and other states.

REVOLUTIONARY REVELATIONS

One visitor to Sarah Bache's home, the Marquis de Chastellux, described what he saw there: "Simple in her manners, like her respected father, she possesses his benevolence. She conducted us into a room filled with work, lately finished by the ladies of Philadelphia. This work consisted of . . . a quantity of shirts for the soldiers of Pennsylvania. The ladies bought the linen from their own private purses, and took a pleasure in cutting them out and sewing them themselves. On each shirt was the name of the married or unmarried lady who made it; and they amounted to twenty-two hundred."

The Daughters of Liberty

There was a certain amount of crossover between the Daughters of Liberty and the Ladies Association of Philadelphia. Reed, Bache, and Martha Washington were all active with both groups. The Daughters of Liberty was established around 1770. It was composed of women who boycotted British goods and made up for them by making their own.

The group was not a traditional organization with officers or a set agenda. It was a loosely banded bunch of women whose goal was to exert their sometimes underestimated power to lessen American dependence on British goods by using their individual skills in a cottage industry style.

Quotations to Live (and Die) By!

"I'VE LEARNED FROM EXPERIENCE THAT THE GREATER PART OF OUR HAPPINESS OR MISERY DEPENDS ON OUR DISPOSITIONS AND NOT ON OUR CIRCUMSTANCES."
—MARTHA WASHINGTON

Some of the Daughters of Liberty were so dedicated to their cause that they would not allow gentleman callers into their homes for themselves or their daughters if they were not sympathetic to the patriot cause.

Women, sometimes joined by men, would gather together on village squares and hold spinning contests which they called "spinning bees." The products they created were called "homespun." Their tactic worked. They made Americans less dependent on British goods and created innovative products in the process.

The women also made bullets, uniforms, and other products for the soldiers and distributed petitions protesting British laws and policies. They may not have been fighting their war on the battlefields, but their contributions helped mitigate British influence in the colonies—in the decidedly ladylike fashion that was the standard at the time.

FEDERAL FACTS

The "daughters" invented new products to replace the British goods they boycotted. One was "Liberty Tea," a concoction made from boiled basil leaves that resembled tea—and was not taxed as such.

INDEX